PRAISE FOR *NOBODY NEEDS TO KNOW*

"A powerful, fierce, and vulnerable memoir that situates the fight for intersex rights against the backdrop of adolescence. Pagonis explores the nuance of bodies—of what it means to have a body as a house— and the ways that society and the medical industry have tried to flatten bodies into one-dimensional ideas. This book is a must-read, and as compelling as it is informative."

—Fatimah Asghar, author of *When We Were Sisters*

"A riveting memoir that illuminates one person's beautiful struggle against a system that denied their truth since birth. *Nobody Needs to Know* is critical to understanding intersex issues, and it's also a striking story of growing up and into yourself. Each page brims with a heart-wrenching honesty and irrepressible spirit that anyone can see themselves in. Pidgeon is changing the world and actively destigmatizing the existence of people who aren't simply male or female. This story inspires an essential process that brings us closer to respecting and appreciating a reality that is not binary and yet is one we all share. Pidgeon is a wonderful human being, a conduit for harmony, and an example of what change and growth can achieve. Please read this book!"

—Indya Moore, actor, model, and advocate

T0006226

"The compassionate rhythm of this compelling narrative carries the pain, confusion, and ultimately power of Pidgeon's life journey with grace. Born with a condition that results in intersex traits, Pidgeon was subjected to multiple surgical procedures as an infant and young child. The veil of distortion and lies to explain these ongoing medical treatments was the product of a well-intended but patriarchal, arrogant medical system. In *Nobody Needs to Know*, the complex traumatic impacts of these interventions are described with a gentle, almost forgiving, patience. As Pidgeon shares the twisting effects of this veil, the inevitable impact on their sense of self and sense of safety in the world is clear. In a supreme example of post-traumatic growth and wisdom, Pidgeon shares their educational and advocacy work, which culminated in Lurie Children's Hospital of Chicago, one of the major academic pediatric medical centers in the United States, making the decision to stop performing non-lifesaving infant genital surgery on intersex children. This is a remarkable book by a remarkable person. I highly recommend it; anyone reading this will come away with an awareness and appreciation of the challenges and beauty of a group of people who are as common in our everyday lives as identical twins or redheads yet are mostly invisible or misunderstood."

—Bruce D. Perry, MD, PhD, principal of the
Neurosequential Network

NOBODY

NEEDS

TO KNOW

NOBODY NEEDS TO KNOW

A MEMOIR

PIDGEON PAGONIS

TOPPLE
BOOKS

Little
a

Published by TOPPLE Books/Little A, New York

www.apub.com

Amazon, the Amazon logo, TOPPLE Books, and Little A are trademarks of
Amazon.com, Inc., or its affiliates.

ISBN-13: 9781542029469 (hardcover)
ISBN-13: 9781542029452 (paperback)
ISBN-13: 9781542029445 (digital)

Cover design by Faceout Studio, Molly von Borstel
Cover and interior illustration by Michelle Der Vartanian
Cover image: © Skylines / Shutterstock

Printed in the United States of America

First edition

*Dedicated to every person, intersex and not,
who has been robbed of their bodily autonomy*

AUTHOR'S NOTE

This book is a memoir, and is drawn from my experience, my memory, and the detailed journals I've kept throughout my life. Some names and identifying details have been changed to provide individuals with privacy. Otherwise, this is my story as I remember it and the truth as I've pieced it together over the years.

A NOTE FROM TOPPLE BOOKS

How do you live your truth when the very existence of your body and self threatens the deeply held beliefs of the patriarchy?

In Pidgeon Pagonis's tender and galvanizing memoir, they detail their youth in Chicago, where their life was a confusing mix of softball, block parties, doctors' visits, and surgeries. On the haunting advice of doctors—*nobody needs to know*—Pidgeon tried to minimize the feeling that something was different.

It wasn't until college that Pidgeon discovered they'd been born intersex and the surgeries and hormone pills they had been prescribed were all an effort to assign a binary gender to a body that defied that categorization. From this realization on, Pidgeon's story becomes a sometimes painful, often triumphant one of reclaiming their truth and fighting to raise awareness and protect young children, like Pidgeon, from unnecessary medical involvement.

Pidgeon is a testament to the power of the human spirit. Their anger and frustration over the past only serve to fuel the compassion and love that shine through every page of *Nobody Needs to Know*. This story is essential to understanding gender and the fight we have to form a more truthful and inclusive concept of gender.

—Joey Soloway, TOPPLE Books editor-at-large

PART I

INTRODUCTION

How do you write about the first time you ruptured?

How do you describe what it felt like when flares began escaping from the fissures? How do I tell you what it was like to witness the onset of my explosion at the age of eighteen?

As my core began to collapse, I stood still in my college dorm room, staring hard into a mirror. My reflection was blurred by outbursts of fiery tears. I used the palm of my hand to pull my hair back, and a fresh tear sailed down the ridge of my cheekbone like a tiny, icy-hot comet. I scanned my features with the acuity of an astronomer, searching for my Polaris amid the mesmeric chaos. A neural meteor shower lit up the valleys of my brain as I processed all the things I had, until that moment, avoided realizing.

My eyes traced my inky, unruly eyebrows, skimmed down the bridge of my father's Hellenic nose, and finally landed on the soft patches of jet-black strands of fur above my lip. I'd been at war with that mustache since fifth grade, when my mother finally let me use her hair removal cream. The blurry telescope I was using to survey the landscape—every facial feature and all the puzzling childhood moments—slowly clicked into focus. A glimpse of something resembling truth materialized.

"They lied to me," I said under my breath. "They all lied to me."

CHAPTER 1

For most of his life, my father struggled with stability. At just eleven years old, he lost the most important thing in his life to stomach cancer: his father. His mother—my yiayia—told me that she felt like she'd lost control of him by the time he was in his teens. After just barely managing to graduate high school—"a miracle," it is said—he spent most of his time with cars. Like his father, he was a self-taught mechanic. Unlike his father, though, he was also a part-time hustler.

He and his friends sometimes made money by stripping car parts for profit. When he wasn't stripping cars, he spent his weekend nights drag racing them in dark alleys. And when he wasn't doing burnouts and banging the clutch to shift gears at just the right moment, he could usually be found at a bar with his friends, their motorcycles lined up next to each other out front, drinking beer and keeping one eye on the pool table for the next sucker whose pockets they could bleed dry.

My father was wild with a good heart. Just a bit misdirected. Tall and sun-kissed, like an olive in the Mediterranean sun. My mom fell for George Pagonis and dropped out of her community college, which just so happened to be across the street from where George lived in his family home. George and Laurie, my mom and dad, were soon wed at St. Nicholas, the church my mom's grandfather helped build—as the story goes—after immigrating to Chicago from Albania. Soon after that, I was conceived.

Sensing her first grandchild might grow up with a father who would either die from a drag-racing accident or be locked away in prison, my yiayia had lunch one day with a church friend. This man, she was told, "had connections," and soon after that lunch, my father had a new job with the City of Chicago's Department of Water Management. Suddenly, my dad had what most blue-collar Chicagoans dream of: a solid, steady union city job with benefits, overtime, and a highly coveted pension.

My yiayia's intervention was perfectly timed because shortly thereafter, my mother discovered she was pregnant again, with my first sibling.

After a year or so at his new job, my dad came home one day, stood in the middle of our Austin Avenue living room, and told us it was time to look for a new house—the kind my parents whispered about in the dark when they thought I was asleep.

They settled on a quaint twin-peaked, copper-brick Cape Cod nestled on the border between the Portage Park and Dunning neighborhoods of Chicago's Northwest Side. Even though the new house was only a ten-minute drive away, I was not happy about leaving. Our home, while not much to look at, had everything I thought we needed. Not only was it just two doors down from a yellow-brick three-flat where a bunch of my aunts, uncles, cousins, and grandparents lived, but it also had a pool! We had a freakin' pool, and my parents wanted to leave it behind for the unknown.

What our white-sided home lacked in beauty and size, it made up for in (that pool!) being so close to family! But it was decided, and we were moving.

I grew to love our new house, but it wasn't quite what my parents had dreamed of. Not at first, anyway. Cute and charming on the outside, our Mulligan Street home was a completely different story on the inside. The bathroom's pink tile was cracked, and the living room had chalky white walls that left residue on my little hands. Dark wood engulfed the other rooms—the paneling, the cabinets, the floors. Peeling yellow-striped wallpaper exposed an underlayer of black paper—remnants of all the families who had lived there before us. There was a crayon-yellow countertop and a stainless-steel sink beside a tangle of old wires where a stove should have been. And by the floorboards, a rathole the size of a fist.

In short, our dream house was butt ugly.

"I swear to God, George, if a rat jumps outa there, I'll kill you," my mother said, standing in the kitchen staring at the hole, her voluminous hair pulled back. My father, with his '80s mullet, muscle tank, and acid-washed shorts, looked unconcerned. I could see my mother's concern during that first walk-through, even though she was trying to hide it. It seemed to be bubbling up inside her chest while the Realtor led us down the hallways, going on about the "potential."

My father was undeterred.

"Once me and the guys are finished with this place, you won't even be able to tell it looked like this," my father said. "It's gonna be friggin' gorgeous."

And he was right.

A few months later, my father made good on his promise and fixed our broken little house. He took a sledgehammer to the walls. Laid cream-colored square tiles over the dark wood and installed milk-white melamine cabinets with honey oak trim. He took down the layers of wallpaper. He even cut out a piece of thick drywall and fastened it over the rathole with strips of joint tape. Our little house that could was coming along. That spring, the four of us moved in—Mom and Dad; my baby sister, Nicole; and me.

We didn't have any family on Mulligan, but I quickly made three best friends—Jennifer, Jenny, and Ashley—and we got a dog named Samantha. The house had a huge backyard where I could get lost amid giant trees that seemed as tall as the Sears Tower.

Soon after we moved in, Mom and I painted decorations on our new kitchen walls. Together, we dipped a scrunched-up paper bag into a tray of mint-green paint before gently smashing it on the wall. "Like this, hun," she said, demonstrating. Then she let me do it, this time with lavender paint and finally with a layer of gold.

While we worked, Mom turned on the stereo to our station—B96. Our favorite song was on—"Pump Up the Jam" by Technotronic—and we really let loose.

Pump up the jam!
Pump it up!
While your feet are stompin'.

My baby sister, Nicole, was asleep in the other room, so the volume was low, and we danced and mimed the lyrics without making a sound. But inside our heads, we were singing at the top of our lungs.

We decorated the kitchen until my father came home from work, and when we were finished, I looked up at Mom through a cloud of cigarette smoke. It was the most beautiful thing we'd ever made together.

❦

When I was five, I'd sit on the floor in the addition that my father built, right next to the curved emerald-green sectional and the gold floor lamp, holding my baby doll. In that living room on Mulligan, I'd pretend that the dolls were my children. I'd dress them up in princess gowns and help them sip their tea—they were fancy little things—before tucking them into bed. I thought playing mommy was what little girls were supposed to do.

On one of those nights, my mother was in the kitchen fixing dinner. She had the phone cradled in the crook of her neck, the cord pulled tight, and was stirring with one hand while hushedly muttering something to my auntie Barbara. Then I heard the thuddy clicking sound that meant she had hung up.

"Jen?" my mom called out.

I let her words hang in the air unanswered.

"Jennifer? Where are you, hun?"

Jennifer. Even then, the name wasn't me. It never felt like me.

The smell of chicken simmering in cinnamon tomato sauce filled the kitchen. My mother was in black spandex with stirrups and a flowy neon tank, her Tina Turner hair pulled back in a banana clip. She was beautiful. She lowered the flame on my favorite Greek dish—chicken and hilopites—and found me in the living room.

"There you are." She sighed. "Didn't you hear me calling your name?"

I looked up from my doll and stared blankly at her. Something was up.

She turned down the Salt-N-Pepa song on the radio. Then she gently took my doll from me and led me by the hand to sit on our emerald-green sofa. Brushing my bangs from my forehead, she smiled, but her smile had a heaviness to it.

"Sit down, hun. I need to tell you something."

Suddenly, our dinner's warm aroma seemed to overwhelm the living room. I glanced longingly at my doll, which was slumped on the corner of the glass coffee table. I wondered if she was hungry too.

My mother took a Marlboro Red out of its pack and balanced it on the edge of her lip. I watched the flame of the gas-station lighter meet the white tip a few times before the cigarette finally caught. She kept her eyes on me, exhaling the smoke out of the side of her mouth.

Then she tried to explain to me, as best she could, what she herself wasn't allowed to fully understand.

"This isn't going to be easy for me to tell you," she said. "But your doctor says you're old enough now." She paused, took another drag, and let the smoke flood her lungs before spilling out into the space between us. "You see your baby over there?" She pointed at my doll.

I looked at my doll again, then back at my mom, wondering what time Dad would be getting home. He loved chicken and hilopites too.

"Hun, when you were born—" Her eyes seemed to be trying to reassuringly smile while holding back tears. "You had cancer in your ovaries," she finally said. "Ovaries are what let mommies create babies.

And cancer . . ." She trailed off. This was serious. "Um . . . cancer is something that's really dangerous and could've killed you."

On the TV, the Rugrats were having a birthday party for Tommy. I was suddenly, unreasonably, jealous of those Rugrats. As far as I could tell, there wasn't an episode in which they had to worry about ovarian cancer.

My mother took another long drag, dabbed the cherry out in a glass ashtray, and continued. She tried her best to use words I could understand, but I was too young to understand, and I zoned out, overwhelmed with a sense of fear and loss that no five-year-old should ever feel. The most primitive dreams I was just forming—the mother I assumed I would be, the family I assumed I would have—all seemed to disintegrate before me. What was clear was that cancer was bad, and at one point I'd had it. It was once in me. I was sick—something inside me was wrong.

I was too young to really remember any of the surgeries I'd had before that conversation. There were trips to the hospital. A few confusing memories that I couldn't understand. But in that moment, I felt as if something were being stolen from me. I later began to understand it was my chance to be a normal kid.

"Hey, hey, listen," my mom said, her voice softer as she consoled me. "You could always adopt a baby."

But that's not the game I'd been playing, the role I was preparing for. Even at five, I knew I wanted to be just like my mother and my auntie Barbara and Gram and my cousin Felicia. I wanted to have my own kids. The "normal" way.

"The doctors saved your life, hun," Mom said, stroking my hair and wiping the warm tears from my face. "It was a miracle. You being alive is a miracle."

I didn't know what to say or feel. I just knew that I trusted my mother. And I was scared. I did my best to keep calm as my mother lit another cigarette and waited for me to respond, but I didn't want to talk. I wanted to run upstairs and hide in my bed under my New

Kids on the Block comforter. Instead, I just stayed there. I couldn't do anything except stare into the vacant eyes of my baby doll as everything else melted away.

❦

About a year before our move to Mulligan Street, we took the first trip that I remember to what was then Children's Memorial Hospital in Chicago. In 1990, Children's was known as one of the best children's hospitals in America, and founded in 1882, it was one of the oldest.

When I was four, the specialists at Children's told my family to schedule me for a procedure. The doctor, I'm told, had observed that my clitoris was one and a half centimeters long. I don't remember much of anything about what happened before the surgery, but my mother has told me that they wouldn't let her come into the operating room with me. She wasn't even allowed to hold my hand as they took me down the hallway. She says I was crying. She says she was crying too.

I do remember that when I got home, my cherished Cookie Monster blanket wasn't with me. Everywhere I went, that blanket went too—I'd sit next to the washing machine and cry when my mother washed it. I told myself it must have been left behind in the recovery room, so when my mom and I went back to the hospital for a follow-up appointment, I made my mom take me to the exact room where I'd recovered a week or so before. My mom went through the motions of asking the nurses nearby if they had seen my blanket, and no one had. When it became clear I wasn't going to get it back, I glared at the boy who now sat in my recovery bed with anger and suspicion. I wouldn't realize until much later that my blanket wasn't the only thing I lost.

After that second surgery, the nightmares began.

In one, I float flat on my back. The ceiling and its fluorescent lights whiz by, one after another, like fluorescent shooting stars. Then my chin kisses the top of my chest, and I see my toes. Everything still whooshes by my feet. I glance down a bit more and see something strange: rolls of

11

toilet paper packed between my upper thighs and soaked in inky blood. That is always the moment I wake up, in the dark, afraid and alone.

My other dream had nothing to do with the hospital. In it, I peek out my bedroom window as tanks roll down my block. Fighter jets fly low over our house, threatening to drop bombs. An invading army is coming. It's a war zone in the streets.

A few months after the surgery, after those dreams began to fill my nights, I woke from a nightmare to the sound of my father's Harley vrooming into the driveway. Outside, the seasons were just changing to autumn. The leaves on the ground were turning red and burnt yellow, cinnamon and cider gold. Headlights illuminated my bedroom, and I sneaked out of my room quietly. My father came in the side door, smelling like beer and burned rubber. My mother was sitting in the dark in a white metal kitchen chair, her back against the wall, waiting. Her arms were crossed.

"Where were you?" she asked.

"Out with the guys," he said.

"You missed your daughter's performance. Again."

I jumped in. "It's okay, Daddy!"

My mother shot me a look that told me now wasn't the time.

"I'm sorry, baby," he said to me, steadying himself on the countertop. "Daddy's gonna make it up to you. I promise."

"You think it's nice for your daughter to see you like this?" my mother said.

"Relax, Laurie, will you?" he slurred. "Jesus Christ."

"No, you relax, George!" Her voice grew louder, echoing off the walls. "I can't take this anymore."

There was a lump in my throat. I looked down at a dark speck on our white kitchen table as everything around me began to melt away.

Around the time I started going to the hospital, I began to hear my parents yelling through the walls. Was it about me?

My cheeks reddened, and it became hard to breathe, and even harder to swallow.

My father yelled back: "*You* can't take this anymore? I bust my ass every day for you to sit around and bitch and moan. *I* can't take this anymore!"

I sprinted up the stairs two at a time and threw my comforter over my face, squeezing it tight as the dam broke. The floor beneath my bed rumbled, as if a tank had plowed through our kitchen. I heard a crash, more screaming and yelling, and my own teary, snotty gasps as I tried to pray. "Please, God, make it stop. Please make them love each other. Please . . ."

And they tried.

That summer, I rode in the annual block-party parade on my pink-and-green Huffy without my little-kid training wheels. I saw my parents in the crowd, my dad cracking open his Budweiser and giving me a thumbs-up. I beamed at their approval.

"Baby Got Back" was blaring from the DJ's speakers. My friends and I giggled as we raced each other to the blue wood barricades, the words CITY OF CHICAGO stenciled on them in white spray paint, at the end of our block. Families brought their giant bowls of potato salads and jiggly Jell-O molds to the tables in the street and cheered us on as we paraded up and down. Things felt normal.

A few weeks after the parade, my parents sat me down on the tattered green sofa one more time. This time they told me that our family was broken.

They were getting a divorce.

"He's still your father, no matter what," my mother said.

"It doesn't change nothing, baby," my father chimed in. "I still love you and your mom very much. Mommy and Daddy just won't be living together in the same house anymore."

"This isn't your fault," my mother said. "Some parents just work out better as friends."

I was sad for Nicole and myself but also kind of relieved. I'd spent a lot of time terrified beneath the blankets while they argued, hyperventilating under the covers, soaking my mattress with tears. I hoped the divorce would mean that this scary chapter was over.

"And one more thing, hun," my mother said. "We are going to sell the house."

That hurt. I looked at my father in disbelief, and he was looking down. I began to cry.

"But where will we live?"

"We're going to stay at Gramma and Grampa's house. Just for a little bit until we figure things out. Just for a little while."

"Where's Daddy going to live?"

"I'm getting an apartment," he said. "And you can visit anytime."

In the weeks that followed, we said goodbye to the house on Mulligan. We packed all our belongings into used boxes we got from the grocery store down the street, boxes that smelled like overripe bananas and stale coffee. I don't remember the day we left. I don't remember saying goodbye to my father, or if he was even there. I don't remember the end. But I do remember the pair of burnt-sienna midcentury modern sofas in my gramma and grampa's living room that would, when pushed together at night, become the bed my mom, sister, and I slept in for the next couple of years.

There wasn't a single day I didn't miss our old house. Gramma and Grampa didn't get along. They lived in a three-bedroom apartment and slept in separate rooms. I missed dancing with my mother in the kitchen, playing in the yard, helping my father fix his cars in the driveway. It may not have been much, but it had been ours.

But there were *some* good things about our new life. My teenage cousins lived on the third floor of our apartment building. They loved Michael Jackson and New Kids on the Block just as much as I did. They introduced me to Billy Idol and professional wrestling, and I became obsessed with WWE. I made new friends. Us kids spent all day playing outside: laughing, running around, hopping fences, and skinning our knees on the neighbors' lawns. Some days, I'd refuse to come inside.

"You're worse than your boy cousins!" my mother would yell at me from the back door.

But I'd refuse to stop playing. I loved nothing more than playing. I played every game you can imagine. I pretended to be anyone but myself.

I never wanted to go inside.

CHAPTER 2

The year I turned eleven was one of changeups.

"That's it!" Gram screeched one afternoon while I sat at the dining room table staring off into our painting of the matador with his stormy blue-black bull instead of doing long division. "I've had enough!" she huffed before slamming down her newspaper. Printed in it were details about the lives of the teenagers who had been shot and killed in our alley earlier that week.

Before they were murdered, we awoke one morning to find spray-painted gang signs all over the garages on our side of the alley. The day after, the other side of the alley was tagged. Suddenly, the alley—my long and narrow concrete playlot—had become a quasi-open-air gallery, with works featuring pitchforks, crowns, and scribbly letters and numbers. Apparently, the artists didn't care for each other, because soon after the gallery popped up, so, too, did the bodies. The sewer where my neighbors and I had recently spent an afternoon, attempting to rescue our dropped roller-hockey sticks, was now a reservoir for the blood of two more victims of the city's gang wars.

"I'm calling Mary-Jo!" Gram declared as I snapped out of the bullfight and came back to the room. "Laur! What's Mary-Jo's number?" she hollered to my mother, who was in the kitchen pouring herself a Diet Rite. Mary-Jo was one of my T-ball teammate's moms and a Realtor who liked to hand out her card at games. I looked back at the bull on the wall and imagined his horns inching closer to the bullfighter's gut.

Our 1920s yellow-brick building on Austin Avenue, which everyone just called "the building," loomed over all the smaller single-family homes on the block. I often thought it looked like a castle tower, the kind knights liked to keep prisoners in. It seemed like everyone in my mother's family either currently or had once lived in that tower. The building contained five apartments bursting at the seams with family, friends, and sometimes random strangers. It was Gram and Gramp's house, Auntie Barb's sometime house, blind Uncle Petey's house, my aunts and uncles and cousins' house, and my yiayia's—who spoke Greek and English and Albanian all at once—house. And after my parents broke up, after the house on Mulligan, it became our house.

It's where I did my homework at the kitchen table while Gram simmered green beans and lamb on the stove. Where I laid my head on my mom's lap on the navy-blue papasan chair as she tickled my back and put me in a trance. And it's where Nicole and I played outside all summer long, she with the little girl next door and I with the boys on the block; we'd mimic our favorite wrestlers and play "Olly, Olly, oxen free!" all night alongside the fireflies. It was our hodgepodge of a castle on Austin Avenue, always ready to catch any one of us when we fell. But Mary-Jo helped Gram get rid of it and buy a different building somewhere else, somewhere *safer.*

The new building was a smaller and stouter two-flat built in the 1960s, with none of the charm or character of our previous yellow castle. Located in Elmwood Park, a neighboring village that everyone called EP for short, it was only ten minutes away from Gram's old place on Austin and just a few steps away from the city, but we might as well have time-traveled to a whole other universe.

If an outsider wasn't paying super-close attention to how the street signs and trash cans changed colors upon entering, they probably wouldn't have even noticed that they had left the residential Northwest side of the city. But to me, the differences were stark and immediately palpable.

Everything felt and looked crisper. The grass was neater, the edges of buildings were sharper, and the sky even seemed bluer. It was like my life, except upgraded to HD. Not quite a traditional suburb and also not quite the city, EP blurred the line between the two. It was the type of place that compelled you to stiffen and walk a bit softer. The adults just kept going on about how much safer it was, but I wasn't sold.

Instead, I couldn't shake the feeling that my world was crumbling yet again. After our last move, which *was* outside the borders of our school district, Mom was able to finesse her connections with the staff to keep Nicole and me in the same elementary school. But now that we were in a whole other town, her connections couldn't help us keep up the charade.

One of the first things Mom did after we moved to EP was take my sister and me to our new school, John Mills Elementary, in order to figure out how to get us registered, legitimately, for the upcoming school year. The building was a bit smaller than my old school and was almost completely empty except for a few people working in the office over the summer. Its blaring emptiness and air-conditioned vastness sent a prickly feeling up my spine. To distract myself, I tried to focus on the scents of cleaning products and cafeteria food that lingered in the frigid air.

It smells the same, I thought.

But nothing else was the same. It seemed that every time I got comfortable somewhere, we left and started over. And while there were some good things about the new apartment—like the fact that we now had two toilets instead of one, and my mom, Nicole, and I had graduated from the couch to our very own room, complete with a very cool shared bunk bed—I couldn't shake the dread of what I feared was just around the corner.

Knowing I was about to be the new kid sparked a lot of worries. *Will anyone talk to me? Will anyone make fun of my crooked front teeth and gap? What about my hairy arms or, worse, my hairy legs that had recently become thicker and darker? And what about my mustache? Are they going to say anything mean about it?*

On the one hand, I was telling myself that I didn't need the other kids to like me, and I was going to proudly own the fact that my family wasn't from that village. On the other hand, I was living with the constant fear of *no one liking me*.

I also had a new fear: that, as an isolated loner, I'd never have a boyfriend, which I was too young to even be thinking about. At my old school, I had a crush on Philip Garcia, and now I wondered if the feelings of longing for him would ever cease. The possibility of living the rest of my life heartbroken and alone before rolling over one day to die in Elmwood Park felt awfully tangible.

Nicole and I only hung out with each other in our new backyard that quiet summer, and when it came to an end, we geared up for the new school year. I was entering fifth grade, and Nicole was in first. As was pretty much tradition by that point, my father had promised to pay for some part of our back-to-school clothes and supplies but then backed out when the bill was due. He and my mom argued annually right before the school year. They'd get upset with each other when he dropped us off after taking us out for a hot dog or some ice cream.

It played out in dramatic phone conversations too. "George, you haven't paid child support in how many years? The least you can do is get your kids some school supplies!" my mom shouted into the receiver one evening during the waning summer nights.

The back-to-school bickering meant that my dad sometimes came through at the last minute with some cash. If he didn't, my mom would figure things out by either pulling some extra shifts at work, pawning her wedding jewelry, or—her least favorite way—borrowing money from her family. Everything always felt super stressful right before fall, and that year we had the added pressure of being at a new school.

❧✺❧

As I feared, I sat by myself at lunch on the first day. Sitting alone with my tray of reheated meatloaf and pint-size carton of chocolate milk, I scanned the cafeteria, jealous of all the kids who were laughing together. Their boundless, uninterrupted happiness seemed to only underscore my own loneliness.

But after a few days, a small miracle happened: a group of fifth-grade girls, laughing and walking arm in arm away from the lunch line, spotted me sitting by myself. They sat down beside me and asked why I was sitting alone. I didn't have a good answer for them. But from that moment on, I would never eat lunch alone as a fifth grader.

I have no clue why those popular girls decided to include me in their group, but I wasn't about to question their thought process. I had somehow lucked into a group of friends, and suddenly the school year didn't seem so bleak.

One day at lunch, while sitting with my new group of friends, I overheard Lisa—a tall, lanky dishwater blonde with blue eyes and a bit of acne—mention something that made my ears perk up.

"My dad's friend from work is starting up a new softball team for girls, and tryouts are next week," she said. "He told me to invite my friends."

I was thrilled. I got the details from Lisa and was soon after officially a Chicago Alley Cat.

Softball became my life. I was never happier than when I was out there under the sun, taking signs from my new coach and digging my rubber spikes into the diamond's dirt. My coach's name was Tommy Thompson, but we just called him Coach Thompson, or Coach. He was an Irish-Catholic ironworker with a lightning patch of silver in his hair and matching silver flecks in his otherwise lake-blue eyes. He seemed to subsist only on a diet of gas-station coffee and sunflower seeds.

My dad would often comment that my coach was a "maniac," but he'd always say it with a grin. He did think my coach was *extreme*, as did almost everyone else who ever met him, but he was more or less fond of him. I was fond of him too. With my dad not around as much after the divorce, I gravitated toward my new coach.

I always tried my best to impress him so that I could hear him say those three coveted golden words: "Good job, Pagonis." Softball was a vehicle for approval—from my coach and from my parents, whenever they could get off work to make it to games. But Coach Thompson was always there, every practice and every game. He was a constant in my life, and I was drawn to him the way a moon is drawn to the gravity of a nearby planet. I was jealous of his daughter, Casey, because I wished for a dad like Coach, one who was so involved in softball and her life.

To my knowledge, our ragtag team was Chicago's first twelve-and-under traveling girls' fastpitch softball team—and it was full of girls who loved sports, just like me. It felt like chicken soup for my soul to be part of the team, going to practice year-round, having pizza parties and sleepovers. It was an instant crew. And I was good at it too. Softball, unlike being girly, came naturally to me.

During the spring of '97, I was eleven, and we were playing our biggest rivals. Bottom of the ninth. Two outs. The count was three and two. And there I was, standing on third, trying my hardest not to do the I-gotta-go dance while Coach Thompson shouted his head off.

"I smell blood!" he roared, which in Tommy Thompson–speak meant he wanted us to pounce and finish off our *wounded* opponents.

I had been holding my pee for most of the game. It was beginning to feel excruciating. I thought I was going to burst.

"Pagonis, get ready to hustle!" Coach Thompson muttered through gritted coffee-stained teeth without taking his piercing blue eyes off our batter, to whom he was giving signs. There was no team in the state—or in the country, for that matter—that got him more riled up than our archenemies: the Oak Park Windmills. It was a personal vendetta for our coach; their wealthy suburban organization had effectively banned him from being around their Ivy League–bound daughters. Without that rejection, our scrappy Alley Cats team would have never gotten started. I would have never found the place where I belonged.

Out of the corner of my eye, I watched his elaborate hand gestures, the secret signs that he had taught us over the winter while practicing night after night in St. Ferd's gym on the city's northwest side. He wanted our batter to smack the ball out of the park so I could score and win the game. "If she pops it up, as soon as they catch it, I want you runnin' home like a hobo after a ham sandwich!" he whispered so only I could hear after he finished giving her his signs. I was fast, one of the quickest on the team, and Coach knew it.

I had become addicted to the feeling I got whenever Coach was proud of me. And I can still hear his gruff voice teaching me to field grounders and catch with two hands.

Two hands, Pagonis! Let's go! he would say, his voice bouncing off the walls of the gymnasium. *It takes ten thousand repetitions before it becomes second nature, ladies!*

Softball practice was an escape. It was the place where we could leave our problems behind. In fact, that's exactly what Coach would tell us to do.

Leave all your problems at home, he'd shout whenever it looked like one of us was losing focus. *This is the one place where all you have to think about is playing ball. How lucky you all are!*

Whenever he was teaching us new *mechanics*, new skills needed for the game, he'd repeat another of his favorite phrases: *Fake it till you make it!* That phrase always made me feel kind of weird, partly because I grew up learning that faking things, like lying, was bad, and partly because softball was the one place where I didn't have to pretend. It was the only space where I felt accepted—where all the parts of myself that weren't *ladylike* were celebrated. It's where I could hawk a loogie and not get chastised by my grandmother. I could just be me, and softball became tied to my future dreams. With softball, if I hustled and worked hard enough, then maybe I could get a scholarship to a university, an education, and have a chance at controlling my own destiny.

Our home field was behind Steinmetz High School, the same school my parents had attended, about ten minutes from Gramma and Grampa's place on Austin Avenue. On that August day, the sky was pink and blue and swirled with white, gauzy clouds. Oak trees cast shadows on the patchy grass, and the sun blinded the pitcher as she whipped in a curveball for the final out.

"Strike three," the ump bellowed.

Thank God, I thought. *Now I can finally pee.*

And as soon as we were done slapping hands with the other team, working up our best sportsmanship smiles—*Good game, good game!*—I sprinted inside the school building for the closest toilet. I rushed inside the metal stall, etched with that pointy *S* that everyone, including me, was obsessed with drawing alongside the names of couples on top of *4EVA*. I pulled down my navy shorts and peeled off my sweaty padded sliding shorts, like veneer on my thigh skin. Then, finally free, I squatted above the toilet to finally let out the pee I'd been holding in.

"Uggghhhhhhhhhhh!"

My legs were exhausted, and after what felt like an eternity, waiting for every drop to drip out, I pulled my skintight sliding shorts back up and began the whole process in reverse. But just as I was about to open the stall door, I felt a warm, wet sensation spread between my legs into my underwear and then the stretchy fabric of my sliding shorts. It was pretty warm that day, and we had just played a doubleheader, so I wanted to believe it was sweat. But this had happened before—more than a few times.

I whined as I stepped back toward the toilet and began peeling off the layers again. I blotted my underwear and sliding shorts with another wad of toilet paper, applying pressure to soak up what I could, then tossing the dirty tissue in the toilet.

When I was as dry as I could manage, I washed my hands and dried them with the hand dryer that blew air out about as well as someone with late-stage emphysema. Etched in the white metal casing with what appeared to be a house key were the words:

FRANKIE + BUBBLES

4EVA

I wondered if I would ever have 4EVA with anyone. But now wasn't the time for all that. I shook off the remaining drops of water and then pressed my hands into the fabric of my jersey. I had to tell someone about my pee problem.

My teammate Lisa's dad dropped me back off at home. When I got inside, Mom was down the hall, in the bathroom, wrapped in a towel. She had a Marlboro in one hand and a pair of shiny chrome cutting shears in her other. Mom's eyes were locked on her reflection as she snipped away at her bangs. Clumps of coarse auburn hair fell like feathers into the porcelain sink. Luther Vandross blared on in the background.

"Mom?" I said, half hoping she wouldn't hear me. "Mom?"

"Huh . . . hun?" she asked, never breaking her concentration.

I didn't like talking about my vagina. I was ashamed to even say the word. After all, I was a child of God who attended Sunday school at an old-school Greek-Albanian Christian Orthodox church every week. My vagina wasn't exactly part of normal dinner-table conversation.

Mom was spritzing herself with a bottle of Dolce & Gabbana perfume, her signature smell. The sharp sting of perfume hit my nostrils, and I found it hard to breathe. I fixed my gaze on the square pink floor tiles and began.

"Come hold the mirror up so I can do the back," she instructed me. I picked up the hand mirror from the bathroom countertop and held it behind her head, just to the side, so she could trim the tendrils that fell on the back of her neck.

"This morning," I said, "I peed . . . and um . . . well, pee came out."

She crooked her eyebrow up at me in the mirror, as if to say, "And?" Then she adjusted her towel over her D cups.

"Huh?"

Redness flushed my cheeks. My eyes tilted up.

"Sometimes," I said, "after I stand up, when I'm done peeing, a little bit of extra pee dribbles out into my underwear. And it's annoying."

What I meant was that it was embarrassing, but at some point I had gotten the idea that my life would somehow be better if I didn't show signs of weakness.

Mom's unimpressed stare turned to a look of fleeting panicked alarm before she set her shiny shears down on the pink counter and said, confidently, "Don't worry about it, hun. I'll call the doctor tomorrow on my lunch break."

CHAPTER 3

The morning of my appointment—April 22, 1997—Mom borrowed Gram's champagne Toyota Camry, and we drove way out to the western suburbs for a doctor's appointment at a Children's Memorial Hospital satellite clinic. The clinic was a sleek two-story building made of glass and cherry-red brick. Inside the lobby, Mom signed me in and waited. I was there to have a routine cystoscopy—a fancy word for having a small camera inserted into your urethra and bladder—so the doctors could better understand what was happening. After a few moments, a woman in sky-blue scrubs called out, "Pa-GAH-nis?"

We followed her down a white marble hall and into an exam room. I knew the routine from school checkup appointments: Step on the scale, step off. Blood pressure check. Pump-pump-pump. Pause. Exhale. Thermometer in the ear. Wait for the beep. Low but normal. But this time they made me strip naked and put a smock on. And then they knocked me out.

And there I was: eleven years old and stretched out on an exam table, legs in stirrups, spread like a splayed chicken in a pan before it was about to go in Gram's oven.

Other than discovering my bladder was *quite capacious*, with *a capacity of 600 ccs*, everything else looked fine. Except for one not-so-little problem. The doctor said urine was getting trapped in my *urogenital sinus*.

In other words, there was something wrong with my urethra.

"A ur-eth what?" I asked.

The only Aretha I knew was Franklin.

The doctor told me I would need a minor surgery to fix the kink in my plumbing. They told Mom they would be in touch to schedule the surgery. And they sent us home.

The months between that appointment in April and my next surgery almost a year later zipped by in a blur of school and homework and softball practice.

The morning of the surgery, Mom and I embarked on a journey down Fullerton Avenue. It was morning, dark, 5:00 a.m. I wasn't allowed to eat before my *procedure*, and my stomach yowled like an alley cat. On the drive, the city woke before my sleepy eyes. Newspaper delivery trucks made their rounds. The sky was an eggplant blanket transitioning to lavender. The main building of Children's Memorial was in a wealthy neighborhood called Lincoln Park, nestled near a six-way intersection exactly one mile before Fullerton ended and Lake Michigan began. When we pulled up, the sun was beginning to rise. The sky was now swirls of my favorite sherbet flavor: rainbow. Mom handed her key to the hospital's valet, and we entered through a spinning glass door.

Inside, we got our instructions, put on our badges, and made our way past a mini museum and a gift shop before arriving at the elevators. The delicious smell of Sausage and Egg McMuffins, of buttery, syrupy pancakes, wafted up from the McDonald's in the hospital's basement and through the elevator chute. I felt as if I would starve as we soldiered on. There was a child, with eyes as blank as a sheet of unused paper, sitting in a wheelchair with a nurse. Blue veins ran like coral under the skin of their bald head. Bags of fluid hung beside them, and one had a black skull and crossbones printed on it. My mom smiled at the kid in a way that was meant to be sweet. She put her hand on my shoulder, and I knew what her face was saying: *Be grateful.*

Inside the exam room, I stripped down and changed into the patient smock that, unbeknownst to me, would become my uniform for the next week.

By 6:30 a.m., a bright-eyed, overly chipper anesthesiologist visited me.

"Hi, Jennifer. Nice to meet you! I'll be taking care of your anesthesia during your operation this morning. I'm going to make sure you are super comfortable the entire time. We have a new machine that lets you customize the scent of your anesthesia mask! What's your favorite flavor?"

I mulled over everything she had said for a few moments before answering.

"Grape," I replied. "But like the Bubblicious grape bubblegum."

"Well, unfortunately, we don't have that, but we can mix grape and bubblegum. Would you like that?"

I nodded. *I hope it doesn't smell at all like regular pink bubblegum,* I thought. I was not a fan of that flavor.

"Great! I'll go dial that into the machine and be right back with it for your approval."

Fifteen minutes later, the anesthesiologist was back with a clear mask. The mask had an air-filled tubular pouch running along its edge. She let me take a whiff, and all I smelled was a heavy, gassy stench of plastic, like plastic that was still warm and had just come out of some mold. I began to retch and dry heaved into a bucket that the anesthesiologist held out. We had to switch to plan B, which involved an anesthesia drip and an IV. My eyes were bloodshot. My stomach was in knots with fear.

At 7:15 a.m., Dr. Firlit, a middle-aged man with a well-groomed mustache, ducked his head into the room.

"We're going to get started very soon," he said. "But before we do, I wanted to pop in and let you know that while we were doing your exploratory procedure with the endoscope, we noticed your vagina was a little bit smaller than that of other girls. We think it would be a good idea to make a small incision while you're on the operating table today to make it a little bit bigger—so you can have normal sex with your future husband. Is that okay with you?"

This statement from the doctor felt confusing and mortifying. But I wanted to be normal. Like the "other girls." I nodded.

"Great. And don't you worry, I'm going to take very good care of you," he assured me. When they came to wheel me to the operation, I grabbed my mom's hand and didn't want to let go. The tears started flowing as the doctor turned to my mom and said, "Don't worry, Ms. Pagonis, we'll have her back to you before you know it."

"I love you, hun," Mom said.

"I love you too," I said through the lump in my throat.

Then they wheeled me off to the OR, down the white fluorescent hallway, the lights whizzing by, just like in my recurring nightmare. In the operating room, a tube blew out anesthesia gas near my face while liquid anesthesia dripped into my IV. I was flat on my back. Dr. Firlit looked like he was upside down as he hovered over me.

"Think of a happy place," he said. I closed my eyes and thought of Disney World, a trip Mom took my sister and me on after the divorce. My auntie Barbara brought her grandson, my cousin Nicholas. Nicole, Nicholas, and I had had the time of our lives meeting our favorite Disney characters, like Aladdin and Jasmine, and getting them to sign our gift-shop purchased autograph books. It was our first, and last, vacation together. We were happy. "Now count backward from one hundred."

Before I got to ninety, I felt like I was under our Disney hotel's rushing pool water, freshly plopped off the waterslide, except I didn't come to the surface.

A few hours later, I woke up in a white room. I felt stuck, like my eyelids were glued shut, like my body was waterlogged. I had no idea what had happened. And then slowly the room sharpened into focus, and the haze began to lift. The faint voices, the whispers of nurses, became louder, clearer, stronger.

I heard a nurse's gentle voice: "Jennifer? If you can hear me, please wiggle your fingers and your toes."

I wasn't quite awake yet, but I was no longer asleep. I was still floating somewhere between drug-induced unconsciousness and consciousness, on a hyphen between drowning and breathing, between feeling and numbness, unable to move or speak.

"Jen, hun, it's your mom. Can you hear me? Can you wiggle your fingers and toes for the doctor, hun?"

Slowly, my eyes fluttered open. The world looked like it was behind watery, out-of-focus binoculars. The room was freezing cold. I could see my mother's chin, her narrow nostrils, her hazel eyes looking into mine, and my reflection looking back at me in her wide, black pupils. A look of relief swelled in her eyes the way Lake Michigan's waves swash across the concrete.

"Hi, hun," Mom said. "You're okay. Everything is okay. You're done."

I could see she'd placed her hand on mine, but I couldn't feel it. As I lay there, I remembered an odd fact: that entomologists believe butterflies don't have pain receptors. And I remembered a story about a butterfly farmer who noticed that some of his butterflies would fall forward onto their heads each time they landed. Upon closer inspection, the butterfly farmer realized their abdomens had been eaten by edacious rodents. But the farmer's butterflies were flying, eating, and even mating as if they were intact for up to eighteen hours. For eighteen hours they existed in a liminal space between life and death.

Thankfully, my pain receptors were blocked, so I couldn't feel the truth of what had just occurred. But I also couldn't feel the warmth of my mother's touch.

The nurse's voice came again. "Jennifer, good afternoon. I'm one of your nurses. You did great. I need you to wiggle your toes, though. Can you wiggle them for me? How about your fingers? Can you wiggle those?"

I tried to comply, with all my ninety-two-pound, eleven-year-old might, but I felt like I was stuck in a bathtub full of sopping wet concrete.

"Come on, hun, you can do it. Just wiggle your toesies for your nurse," my mom coached me.

"Once you wiggle your fingers and toes, Jennifer, we can take you to your room so that you can rest," my nurse added.

I hoped, if I ever got there, the room would be warmer. Eventually, my brain was able to will my fingers and toes to do as they were commanded. When I tried to speak, my vocal cords had been rubbed raw and left inflamed by the endotracheal tube that had been snaked down my throat. Instead of words, all that came out was a dry sputtering of coughs and wheezes that sounded like my father's Camaro the time he took its muffler off. Then I started retching again; I can't remember if I threw up on myself or if someone grabbed a bucket quick enough, but all I know is that I couldn't prevent it.

The nurses wheeled me in a transport cart from the recovery room to another white sterile box of a room. My mom and relatives were there with me, but I don't remember any of that. My memory of those moments after the surgery is hazy.

The nurses gave me some Tylenol to cope with the pain—along with an IV that snaked out of my arm.

❦

"When can I go home?" I asked every single human being who popped past my room.

"That's up to the doctor, young lady," one nurse said. "But it should be soon. Maybe tomorrow if the doctor thinks you're ready."

Yet as each day passed, I lay bedridden. The monotony was broken up by my mother's visits. She would sit by my bedside, slowly tickling my arm, being careful to avoid the IV and other things taped to it while we watched television. And every day, the likelihood of being released—a shining beacon of light at the end of a tunnel—seemed further and further away.

The morning after my surgery, I woke with a catheter hanging out of my body. And boy, oh boy, did I hate that thing. It felt alien, this uncomfortable tube tethering me to a bag of my own urine—a nagging reminder of how abnormal I was. My second question every day was if I could have the catheter removed. I got the same answer as when I asked if I could go home. At first, they told me it would come out the next day. Then the next day.

Then the next.

Each day, while lying there bored out of my mind, watching brain-numbing daytime shows on the TV attached to the ceiling in my room, I would hope and pray this was the day—the day someone would finally take out my catheter. But each day—each excruciatingly long day—came and went with the catheter still jammed up inside me. Let me tell you: there's nothing like being tethered to a bag of your own pee at the tender age of eleven to make you feel good about yourself. It was bad enough that I already felt different from every other girl at school. I was flat. I was hairy, like a baby monkey. And I had a mustache to boot. I didn't (and would never) get a period—and now this!

In the days that followed, my mother, my auntie Barbara, my cousins, and my friend Lisa would stop by to visit me and tie gift-shop balloons to the doorknob to remind me I wasn't alone. But soon another routine developed too—one that was more invasive, uncomfortable. At least once a day—sometimes multiple times a day—a group of medical personnel (mostly men but sometimes women) would walk into my room. The leader of the lab-coated ducklings would loudly introduce himself and ask me for a favor. It went something like: "Hi, Jennifer, how are you doing? I'm one of your doctors, and I've come by to—"

I would stop him before he could finish. "Take my catheter out?"

At this, he would chuckle and say, "No, not today. But maybe tomorrow. I'm here to take a look and make sure everything is healing down there. Mind if I take a look?"

Shyly, dutifully, I would nod as if to say, "Go ahead." I didn't feel I had the power to deny a doctor. And besides, healing was important. The sooner I healed, the sooner I could go home. And then, with a plastic grin plastered on his face, he'd ask, "Do you mind if my residents also take a look with me today?"

Again, I nodded. My body prepared for what was coming by tensing up. I wanted to separate the lower half of my body from the upper, like I had seen David Copperfield do so many times on TV.

The lead lab-coat-wearing duckling removed my blanket and hiked up my gown. They could see everything, my most private parts. He then asked me to spread my legs, which I did, staring at the oscillating fluorescent ceiling light, wishing I were somewhere else, anywhere else. I would stare so intently, so hard, and with such force that everything except what was directly in front of me would fade away, David Copperfield be damned.

I kept telling myself it was okay, that by putting myself on display like this—like a science experiment, like a zoo animal—it would help other patients with bladder problems like mine. I kept telling myself it would get me home sooner. I told myself to do whatever it took to get through it.

Had I known what the surgeons had really done to me a few days prior, when they "fixed my bladder," I'm not sure I would have been able to handle it. Instead, I went through the motions. Coach's advice—fake it until you make it—seemed appropriate here. In faking that I was okay, that I was strong and not bothered in the least by the doctors' invasions of my privacy—their daily inspection of my most intimate parts—I was *being strong*. In fact, I was practicing how to shut down every time anyone looked or touched me down there. But to their physicians' eyes, I was being fixed. I was healed. I was whole. I was becoming normal. No one would ever have to know the truth.

Over a week after my surgery, they still hadn't removed my catheter, and I ended up being discharged with it still inside me—roping me like an umbilical cord to the hospital—and a bag of my own pee on my lap as we drove home.

When I arrived home with my mother that day, the apartment felt the same. Everything was in its rightful place: My grandfather was there, in his robe and slippers, smoking his cigarettes in the corner. The mundane sounds of injury-lawyer commercials came blaring from the kitchen TV. "We can help you!" the lawyers promised, as they always did. But I felt different.

I was sore.

My weak legs wobbled as I made my way down the hallway. I went into the bathroom and locked the door behind me. I twisted on the bathtub nozzle, tested the water to make sure it was warm, and carefully removed my clothing as the tub filled. I grabbed the sides of the tub and slowly lowered my body into the water the way my nurses back at Children's had instructed me. Sharp, stinging pain seized my body as my legs attempted to adjust to the heat. I lay there with my head resting against the tile and my eyes closed. As I descended under the water, I glanced up to make sure my bag of pee remained safely above my bladder, just as the doctors had told me to. "We don't want air bubbles in your catheter going inside of you, okay?" they'd cautioned. After taking a deep breath, I spread my legs and reached between my thighs to feel what the doctors had done. But all I could feel were ridges of stitches and flesh swollen around the catheter tube.

Whatever was there wasn't me. Or if it was me, it was a new me. A me I wasn't familiar with.

The feeling turned my stomach, and I shut my eyes tightly. I didn't want to think about it. In my mind, I was back on the softball field. I could smell the fresh-cut grass. I could hear the crack of the bat. I could hear my teammates cheering me on as I hit a home run into left field. I could hear Coach Thompson yelling for me to *dig, dig, dig*.

I was still just a normal girl playing softball. The crowd was chanting my name. And the whole team was waving me home.

CHAPTER 4

A year after my third surgery, I began junior high at Elm Middle School. Elm, as we called it, had two feeder elementary schools that both coalesced into one middle school for the seventh and eighth grades. And seemingly overnight, all my friends had mutated into gawky, hormonal, acne-covered, menstruating beauties. Every girl in the seventh grade seemed to be changing. Everyone, that is, except for me.

I wasn't hormonal. Or sprouting. Or breaking out. And I certainly hadn't obtained the holy grail of full-blown womanhood: the coveted period. My friends not only had gotten their periods but were all registering impressively on the breast spectrum. Karie—the most beautiful girl in my grade—had already achieved a perfect C cup by sixth grade. Now others were catching up or surpassing her.

And then there was me: a skinny, flat-chested, crooked- and gaptoothed, frizzy-haired, brownish student. I was the one they called Bic—yes, after the razor blade company—because of the coarse black hair that graced my arms, my legs, and—most dreaded—my upper lip. It wasn't the type of nickname that did wonders for a preteen psyche. Nor was it the only nickname I had either. My ethnicity is Greek, Albanian, and Mexican. When I shared that information, some of my classmates would pick on me by calling me a "spic" and a "wetback." My previous school was more diverse, and the kids there weren't belittled for being Mexican or Puerto Rican. They were the cool kids, and I always was proud of my Mexican heritage; in fact, I wished I were even more Mexican. Hearing the insults from my new classmates made me regret I'd ever told the kids I was part Mexican. It made me want to hide in yet another way. Any perceived difference from the norm was now grounds for bullying. Racial epithets were hurled at Brown students, and "flat-chested bitches" was spat at girls with A cups—or less. It seemed as if everything about me—those things visible and not—was a vulnerability waiting to be exploited by fellow students. Every moment in my body felt excruciating. Whenever the topic of periods came up—which it did, roughly 364 times a day—I would use my swift chicken legs to dash out of the conversation. "Oh, look," I'd say, creating a diversion, "there's a lonely little book in the library about bearded dragons that wants to be read." And I'd sneak off, far, far away from the topic of menstruation.

I lied to all the girls about not getting my period for as long as I could. Soon, I had told so many different period tales to so many different friends, I couldn't keep my stories straight. For most of seventh grade, I lived in fear of being found out—that I'd been lying about one of the most sacred things there is: periods! It was all too much to bear. I couldn't take it anymore! It was just a matter of time before I was found out. I never felt comfortable. My lungs began to tighten. My shoulders were forever tense. My digestion stalled to a standstill.

I prayed so many nights to God to give me a period, religiously checking for bloodred stains on the fabric of my panties each time I pulled them down to use the bathroom. I prayed for my boobs to grow. "God, are you there?" I'd ask. "Could you spare a simple A cup for a girl in need? Or, maybe if you're feeling generous, a C?" But I knew it was futile. My mom had already told me years ago that my girl parts were broken from the cancer and I would never have a period. What she didn't tell me, or what she didn't quite understand, was that no period also meant no puberty. I was realizing that little tidbit of information on my own. And no puberty meant no normal. But that's exactly what I wanted: to be a normal, pubescent girl.

One day, after softball practice, I heard my friend Clara talking about a sleepover she was having that weekend. Those invitations had become a source of terrible anxiety. Sleepovers, I imagined, were where all the girls would get together and talk about their boobs and first kisses. I hadn't had either. I wanted so desperately to go to one, to be one of the girls, but I knew if I wanted my first junior high sleepover to be a success, I'd need to snag a boyfriend, get that kiss, and hatch a scheme to kick-start my body into puberty.

I had a lot of work to do.

Somehow, even without a C-cup rack, let alone an A, I had already managed to find a boy who liked me. His name was JP—short for John Paul—and he had the cutest dimpled smile, chestnut-brown eyes, and a mushroom bowl cut. He was perfect to me. We even had the same initials, which practically meant we were soulmates in middle school logic. We spent a lot of time passing notes to each other behind our teacher's back with "JP + JP = 4EVA" written on them.

I was going to get that first kiss.

A few weeks into our relationship—just a few months into seventh grade—step one of my plan commenced. JP and I went on a group movie date that included some of my closest friends: Stephanie; her boyfriend, Jimmy; Lisa and Karie; and JP and me. Just after dark, Steph's mom dropped us off in front of the movie theater. It was a cold winter dusk, and the Cinemark marquee lit the sidewalk around us. I felt small, and underdeveloped, standing there with the others between the massive parking lot and the oversize theater. JP, ever the gentleman, offered to buy my ticket.

"We're on a date, after all," he said, eyes sparkling, a playful grin spreading across his face. We had arrived to see *Titanic*. Unchaperoned. This was big! *The perfect movie*, I thought, *for the perfect first kiss*. I was overjoyed, not only to have made a solid group of friends who carried over into junior high but also to have a boyfriend who was as cute and sweet as JP.

We waved goodbye to Steph's mom, and as soon as her silver van was out of sight, Steph and Jimmy began holding hands. JP reached for mine. My palm instantly became a swamp of nerves.

Then the embarrassment of my swamp palm brought on a wave of stabbing cramps—the kind caused by excruciating gas. I felt like I had swallowed a twisted balloon animal. From that point forward, every one of my movements was made with the utmost clenched vigilance.

The six of us spilled loudly into the theater lobby and made a bee-line for the candy. My family didn't believe in spending exorbitant sums of money on overpriced movie theater food and candy. In my family, whenever we went to the movies, my mom and Auntie Barbara would take my sister, my cousins, and me to the corner store, where we'd stuff the pockets and inner linings of our pullover Starter jackets with all the chips and candy and juice we could fit. Then, like a family of Michelin Men, we'd file into the theater, skipping the concession lines, and head straight to our seats to enjoy the film and our contraband.

Since JP bought my ticket, I still had some cash in my pocket. The thought of possibly purchasing an official concession from the theater slightly thrilled me, though after a few quick glances at the prices, it quickly became apparent why my family did what we did. Eight bucks for a box of peanut M&M's? Are you kidding? My relatives raised me better than that. The only thing I had enough cash for was a small popcorn, but I didn't even like popcorn.

"Would you like anything, baby?" JP asked me, snapping me back from thinking about whether he had noticed my slippery palm. It was the first time he had called me "baby" out loud, in front of people.

I was giddy, electric.

I nodded shyly and pointed at the Sour Patch Kids behind the glass. He pulled out a Velcro wallet and handed over a fresh twenty-dollar bill. That's right: not only did my man have a wallet, but there was real, actual money in it! I felt like the luckiest girl in the world. It was right then that I decided I wanted to marry JP, and that night was going to be the night I kissed him. My nerves flared up. The rubber balloon animal squeaked excitedly inside my stomach.

Down, boy, down! I mentally barked back.

Inside the theater, JP sat beside me. The lights went down, and the movie began. An hour later, Jack was holding Rose, the two of them balanced on the bow of the ship. Rose's gorgeous red ringlets framed her angelic face. And handsome Jack, with his adorable mushroom cut, looked kind of like JP. I was enthralled. In fact, I had gotten so swept up in Jack and Rose's love story, I had almost forgotten about my mission.

I had to focus.

Jack asked Rose to trust him, braced her from behind, and told her to spread her arms, up and out. *This is my moment,* I thought. *When Rose opens her eyes, I'm going to make my move.*

The butterflies swelled. Gas was percolating in my belly. I closed my eyes and held my breath. Leaned over. Leaned in. Paused for just a second. And then I did it. I lurched forward and kissed my JP on the cheek.

Adrenaline was coursing through my body. When my lips left his cheek, I immediately stood up and sprinted out of the theater and into the lobby, where I began pacing the neon patch of carpet between the NBA Jam arcade game and an air hockey table. I couldn't believe it had happened. I had just had my first kiss—kinda—with one of the cutest boys in the entire school. I smiled as I tried to catch my breath. I couldn't wait to go to a middle school sleepover. I'd done it. I couldn't wait to tell all the other girls that I had kissed JP.

As it turns out, JP + JP didn't = 4EVA.

Despite having scribbled our love's insignia on every notebook, bathroom door, and bus seat we could get our hands on, we somehow broke up a few weeks later.

I was devastated.

I couldn't see any way for life to go on. I imagined my heart would never heal. I would never be able to find joy in anything, or anyone, ever again.

But, luckily, thanks to a combination of time, softball, school, and friends, life somehow continued. Shortly after JP and I broke up, my mom made another doctor's appointment for me, this time for hormone replacement therapy (HRT)—pills, I would later find out, that would help launch me into puberty.

The morning of the doctor's visit, my stomach was a tangle of nerves as Mom took the familiar Fullerton Avenue to the hospital. An hour later, we were inside the hospital lobby. Unlike at the last appointment in the suburbs, before my bladder surgery, there were no invasive cameras. But just like last time, it was a lesson in the emerging fact that my body was not my own.

After checking in, I sat in the windowless exam room, waiting for close to an hour before Dr. Silverman finally knocked. He was a mustachioed middle-aged white man, draped in a white lab coat, with a stethoscope around his neck.

"Hi, Jennifer! I'm Dr. Silverman!" he exclaimed as he extended his hand to me for a shake. His hand had thick patches of hair between the knuckles and completely enveloped mine. His cheerful demeanor felt rehearsed.

"It says here you play softball?" he said, peering down at his chart. "What's your favorite position?"

"Shortstop," I said.

"Oh, we have our very own Derek Jeter," he said. His nurse chuckled. I was a die-hard White Sox fan, so I preferred Ozzie Guillén, but I didn't say anything.

"Let's have you hop up on this exam table for us so we can take a look-see," he said.

I did as he said. I placed my foot on the slide-out step, then twisted around to sit.

"Your mom tells us you've been asking her questions about puberty?"

I looked down and nodded to signal he was correct.

He then told me that I wouldn't be able to experience natural puberty. But luckily for me, he could prescribe medicine that would help.

As soon as he said this, I immediately began daydreaming of the boobs I hoped would grow as a result of these magic pills. But first, he said he needed to take another *look-see*.

"Can you lie down and lift up your shirt for me?"

I was a teenage girl who had never been intentionally, consciously naked in front of anyone besides maybe my mom and my gram. I gulped and did what he said. I was so embarrassed by the way my white cotton training bra hovered uselessly over my flat chest. But I was even more embarrassed and ashamed by what happened next.

"Okay, now I just need to move your bra out of the way in order to take a peek," he declared. I just lay there. Small, frozen, helpless. Eyes wide. Unable to speak. I told myself to stay focused on the possible prize: boobs. My reward, at last, for all those nights I'd spent lying in bed and praying to God for normalcy.

Dr. Silverman used the pads of his big cold paws to press into the goose-bumped skin on my tender rib cage. He pressed two of his ice-cold fingertips into my nipple skin. I felt a tinge of nausea bloom in my stomach. He did the same to the other nipple, which made me feel even sicker. Once he finished my chest exam, he reported back to his nurse.

"Okay, Jennifer. Now I need you to pull your underwear down to your ankles so I can take a quick look there as well."

Again, I did as he told me. If this was a routine examination, it was not routine to me.

I lifted my pelvis, bridged up, and shimmied my Thursday panties down. I clutched the tops of my thighs for dear life in a fruitless attempt to reclaim a modicum of modesty. Then Dr. Silverman asked me to spread my legs. Against my better judgment, against everything I had been taught about my body, I capitulated. I closed my eyes and opened my legs. He placed his freezing fingers on my vagina and spread it open. I could feel the curved ridge of his nail through the latex glove. My breathing hastened, and my chest, covered again by my puckered bra and T-shirt, was heaving up and down. What happened after is a blur because my body and mind attempted to protect me by shutting down the central command station of my emotions. I tried to be anywhere but in that room, anywhere but in my body.

"Okay, all done," Dr. Silverman said.

He peeled his gloves off. I pulled my underwear up.

"Well, Jennifer, everything looks great. I see no reason why you can't start your medication. I'm going to prescribe you a pill called Premarin."

Premarin was a female hormone that would help launch me into puberty. He told me that if I took just one pill a day, I would begin to see the changes I had always hoped for. His promise wasn't specific. I'd been hoping that my chest would grow.

"Do you have any questions for me?" he asked.

Now that he asked, I *did* have questions: Would I seem normal to a boyfriend? Would sex be normal for me? But I didn't have enough courage to ask.

Instead, I just asked something safe.

"Are the pills chewable?" I asked.

"No, sadly, they're not, but they are very small and easy to swallow," he replied.

Then his facial expression popped the way a clown's does when they show the audience that a new thought has appeared in their head.

"Which reminds me: These pills are *your* business. Nobody needs to know about them except you and your family."

I scrunched my eyes at his peculiar advice, trying to see through the mist of his words.

"You know how kids can be," he said in an attempt to clarify.

I was still not connecting the dots.

"You don't want to give anyone a reason to gossip, right? Kids can be mean. Everything we talked about today, your medical history, is your private information, and no one else needs to know."

Before I hopped off the exam table, he asked me once more if I had any other questions. I was embarrassed to ask the question I really wanted to know the answer to. It made me feel dirty and ashamed, but like a ball from a cannon with a lit wick, it just shot out. I pointed at my chest.

"Will my . . . um . . . will . . . the pills make . . . um . . . these grow?"

I felt like I was going to pass out as I waited in desperation for his answer.

He nodded.

"You should definitely see breast development. Breast tissue growth is one of the medication's effects."

I let out a huge sigh of relief and felt like maybe, just maybe, everything I had just gone through would all be worth it.

During the car ride home, I couldn't stop fantasizing about my *breast development*. I imagined that all my problems would instantly vaporize as soon as I was able to fill out my bra. I would finally have what I wanted more than anything: a visible marker that I had gone through puberty. I would be able to tell the girls at sleepovers that I had kissed a boy and gotten boobs. I would be desirable. I would be like them. I would be normal.

That winter, after I started taking the Premarin, I checked my chest every morning for development. Each morning I was disappointed. All I saw were two tiny breast buds developing behind my increasingly sensitive nipples.

A few weeks later, my friend Clara invited me to her house for an epic sleepover. Clara was one of the first kids I connected with at Elm who was from the other feeder school. When I found out she was adopted, the words seemed to echo in my head. I remembered that conversation my mom had had with me in our Mulligan Street living room way back when I was only a little kid—the one about cancer and babies. Clara was the only adopted kid I knew, and in her I searched for proof that adopted babies could grow up to be happy, to feel loved. During that long-ago conversation, my mother had made it clear that the only way I would ever be a mother was if I adopted. I needed to know adopted kids could be happy. That a family with an adopted child was capable of the same kind of bond and love.

The truth was, I still didn't feel excited about the prospect of adopting. Knowing that I'd have to adopt a child instead of creating one of my own just seemed to underscore the fact that I was too broken to ever really be loved by anyone. I'd developed a fear, which seemed to have taken up permanent residence in a hollow nook inside me, that if I ever found someone who really loved me, he would run from our relationship faster than the Looney Tunes Road Runner when he found out the truth about who I really was, about how I was different. Like the doctor had said, nobody needed to know, but the pressure to keep my secret was taking a toll on me.

Clara, however, seemed to challenge my notion that adoption was embarrassing or shameful. I had been waiting for a sleepover so I could prove how normal I was, so I could experience a moment in which I fit in with my classmates, but going to Clara's also presented me with the opportunity to see if her adopted life was all that it seemed to be from a distance.

With this monumental night approaching, I practically begged Dr. Silverman to increase my dose during my next appointment, but he refused. I hadn't given up on my dreams of big, Karie-size boobs, ones that all the boys would drool over, but each day that dream was becoming harder to hold on to.

That weekend, a van honked out front of my house. My ride was outside, and as usual, I wasn't ready. I packed my translucent-orange bottle of puberty pills in a rolled-up pair of socks, which I tucked under my comfy plaid pajama pants in the deepest corner of my softball duffel bag. I quickly zipped up my bag, jumped into my shoes, slung my bag over my shoulder, and sprinted to the pink bathroom to take a quick glance in the mirror before making my way out the door.

"Bye!" I shouted to my mom as I slammed the door shut and cleared the entire landing of stairs with one huge leap that almost broke my knees on the way down and out of the building. I stuffed my toothbrush in my pocket and opened the van door.

"Bye, hun!" my mom shouted from the front window, the screen obscuring her face. "Don't stay up too late!"

"I won't!" I yelled back, pressing the button that made the van door close like magic.

Here we go, I thought to myself. *This is it. The night I've been waiting for.*

Clara's house was on the other side of the tracks—both literally and figuratively. As soon as you got south of the train tracks in EP, you could see the neighborhood become more affluent, a bit more white collar, cleaner. Some of the parents on the south side of Elmwood Park were dentists and lawyers, and some of them were even country club elites. Clara's family wasn't like that, though. Her dad worked for the village as a street sweeper, and her mom was a beautician. Her house was a modest, one-story brick home with a finished basement—the basement that would become the scene of my very first middle school sleepover.

Clara was an only child, had a cute cherubic face, and always sported the best highlights and layers in her ringleted hair. I always loved being able to see other people's homes. Clara's smelled like Yankee Candles, basil, and garlic. Even though she was adopted, she looked just like her Italian parents. Nobody could even tell. Stephanie and Lisa made their way to the kitchen and then down to the basement. I hung back and took it all in. Clara's bedroom door was open. I peered in and saw that it was perfect. A room of her own, full of scrunchies and lip gloss and butterfly clips. Pictures of her family and friends, alongside keepsakes like concert ticket stubs, bulged out of one of those upholstered memo boards, the kind with crisscrossing ribbons forming Xs.

Other smiling photos were framed on her dresser and nightstand. She looked so happy.

Clara's mom was in the kitchen in the back of their home.

"Hi, hun, how's your mom?" Linda asked me.

She called her daughter's friends "hun," like my mom. Both she and my mom had similar haircuts too: the short one with bangs that every mom seemed to have at the time. I felt comfortable.

"Oh, she's good," I replied. "She told me to tell you hello."

"You can go on down," she said with a warm smile. "The other girls are already down there. Have fun tonight."

And with that, I descended into the subterranean world of teenage sleepovers. The other girls were already in their pajama pants and over-size tees, gossiping about our classmates and talking about Matt and how cute he was.

"Oh my God, his dimples!" someone squealed. (He did have great dimples.) Even better than JP's. Matt was everything. I'd seemingly entered this party at the exact right time. I had a huge crush on him—the kind where I had taken a picture of him, folded it up, and slid it into a clear plastic photo sleeve attached to a ridiculously small pillow. Stephanie had gotten it from the mall and gifted it to me one year for my birthday. It was the most uncomfortable pillow that ever existed, made of cheap neon-green-and-purple faux fur and stuffed with hard Styrofoam beads, but I didn't care. I would lie on it and dream of Matt and his perfect dimples.

"Maggie and Matt, sitting in a tree . . . K-I-S-S-I-N-G!" Clara sang out loud as she teased Maggie, another of our friends at the sleepover. Everyone joined in. I did my best to join the chant, but at the pit of my stomach was a bowling ball of jealousy. I wasn't the only one with a crush. Maggie had beach-wavy blonde hair, blue eyes, and a megawatt smile. She looked perfect even when she was in her usual jeans and an oversize hoodie. She had an effortless coolness about her, a confidence that I could only dream of, and she was both everyone's best friend and everyone's dream girl. We played softball together for our junior high team at Elm, and she was just one of the prettiest, coolest, funniest people on the team. I was enamored with her, and now, apparently, my crush was too.

When I realized that Matt and Maggie were dating—seventh grade's newest power couple—I tried to maintain a tough exterior. I must have been delusional to think Matt would ever date me in the first place. Matt was tall and athletic, with a chiseled jawline. He was the most popular boy in the entire seventh grade. Oh, and those dimples. (Have I mentioned his dimples?)

Hearing about their relationship reminded me of everything I was there to forget. I was the flat, hairy, chicken-legged girl. Who would want a chicken that couldn't even lay eggs? I held back my tears.

Hours later, lost in our sugar-filled, sleep-deprived delirium, we all got a case of the giggles. That's when Clara got the idea that we should all flash each other. *What did she just say?* The energy in the basement shifted, and I could feel a sense of nervous excitement in the air.

I was terrified.

My boobs had only just started growing, and I hated how pubescent my nipples still looked. I had seen my mom's breasts and nipples; I'd seen my aunts' and grandma's. Mine looked nothing like theirs. Theirs were so real and mature in a way I couldn't describe. I thought of my new tiny boobs as artificial; they were only possible with pills—pills I had hidden in the deepest corner of my overnight bag. My face and chest became hot, flush with anxiety over what was about to happen.

In a giddy whirlwind, each girl took turns showing the group their boobs.

Maggie went first and flashed us two beautiful, round, perky boobs. Her nipples were light pink. Almost translucent. And stood perfectly at attention in a way mine hardly ever did. My shame only intensified. After a few seconds, she then pulled her bra back on, one breast at a time, and then tugged her shirt back down. Something about this move underscored that she was the comfortable owner of an enviable rack. I had a long way to go.

The others went next.

One by one.

One perfect set after another.

Clara was the only one who seemed a bit ashamed. "My nipples are really big and weird," she told us as she bit her lip before showing us.

They *were* really big, and the edges weren't well defined like the others', seeming to just blend into the rest of her breasts. Even then, I would have done anything to swap with her.

After Clara, there was only one person left: me.

I fidgeted with my shirt. Bit my lip. Everyone's eyes were on me. My breath became shallow as the seconds ticked by, until I realized I wasn't breathing anymore. I hoped if I held my breath long enough, I would just disappear. Everyone's boobs were so perfect, so amazing, and I couldn't bear to show them mine. I was too ashamed.

The pills and the cancer were my secrets. *Nobody needs to know,* I thought to myself. But I wanted so badly to tell them the truth. I wanted to tell them everything I'd been going through.

Hiding the pills, hiding the doctor's visits—it was too much. Living in fear and having so many conflicting stories about my first period. Thinking that I was the only girl in the room who couldn't grow up and have a baby. It all sucked the air out of the basement. I was suffocating.

Then I did something reckless. I blurted out that I would never get my period and could never have children. I could hear every tick of the clock that was tacked up on the basement wall. I was coming close to entering a black hole. *Oh no, I wasn't supposed to do that. I wasn't supposed to tell anyone, and now I just told everyone.* Before I crossed the horizon line into oblivion, I quickly laughed it off as a joke.

"I'm just messing with you," I lied.

There was an awkward pause.

"Are you gonna flash us or not?" Clara asked.

I closed my eyes.

My heart thumped in my chest, and I clenched my teeth; the weight of the shame and my secrets bottlenecked in my chest as I stood there in front of them.

My jaw tightened. My face flushed red.

And then I opened my eyes.

"No," I said. "I can't."

CHAPTER 5

Two years later, on the first day of high school, dozens of girls in scratchy red sweaters went scampering through the halls of my new Catholic high school—Trinity.

I was nervous but excited to have a fresh start. My middle school experience had been two terrifying years of learning Spanish, plodding through math class, and feeling that I was ugly. After the failed Operation Sleepover, my anxiety over not fitting in only swelled.

For the entire summer before high school, I was floating in an ocean of delusional hope—that one day I'd wake up, birds chirping, and look down to see miraculous boobs propping up my oversize tee and period blood staining my white Ikea sheets. Those few months of sunshine and humid skies felt like my last chance to *develop*. The thought of bearing another chapter of my life as the odd one out had me feeling desperate.

The day before school started, I wasn't able to get a single second of sleep. Up all night with first-day jitters, I was also being crushed by the realization that my hopes and prayers had gone unanswered. The hormone pills Dr. Silverman had prescribed to me had kicked in, but the results were disappointing. The boobs I ended up with weren't the showstoppers I had hoped they would be. Sure, I wasn't flat anymore, but my new itty-bitties weren't enough to distract from what I perceived to be my body's awkward shortcomings: my mustache and lanky legs and underdeveloped no-hip-having frame that just wouldn't fill out. The magic pills, as it turned out, were duds. My prayers were lost in the mail.

Father, why have you forsaken me?

There were rumors that the all-girls school Trinity was full of lesbians. So when I arrived that first day, I was expecting a frumpy lesbian oasis ruled by pious nuns in habits. But it quickly became obvious, in the sober light of morning, there were few, if any, lesbians.

A good portion of the girls were image obsessed, in hyper-posh, chunky-heeled patent-leather Mary Janes, their skin tanned to a honey glow and their blown-out hair reeking of perfume and drugstore hair spray.

In the mornings, the bathrooms were full of teenage girls in white button-ups and plaid wool skirts slumped over the sinks, drawing on their eyebrows and pursing their lips while they slathered on sparkly MAC lip gloss. The hallways were choked with Bath & Body Works' Cucumber Melon body spray, and girls rushed past me, staring blankly into their compacts.

I'd heard the refrain *High school is gonna suck* over and over again from the kids who weren't slated, like me, to attend a single-sex Catholic high school.

"Have fun with all the dykes," Chris, the same boy who called me Bic in junior high, liked to sneer.

There was a reputation that struck real fear into high schoolers' hearts: that going to a single-sex school was a kind of punishment. The death of their social life. That only the girls going to coed schools would have typical high school experiences. What would it be like with no boys there? Whatever would we do with no boys?

Looking back, I hate that I was this obsessed with boys, but I was short on other forms of validation. At some point during the previous handful of years, I had begun believing that the roots of my self-worth were extraneous: grades, sports achievements, and boys' desire. I was concerned my social life, the one I had fantasized about the entire summer to distract me from the gut punch that was junior high, the one I had dreamed about while watching rom-com couples canoodling in their high school hallways, was dead. All I could focus on was what I thought I was losing—the chance to have the classic high school experience: homecoming, football games, and dating boys.

I couldn't yet appreciate what an all-girls school afforded me. I wasn't wise enough to realize how so much of the devastating lack I felt within my body was linked to being enmeshed in the social dynamics of a coed school environment, where many of us girls got swept up in a cutthroat competition with one another for the boys' attention. Where when girls who didn't have big boobs stood up to teasing boys, they were called flat-chested bitches—a stark warning to the rest of us. Teenage girls rarely get to be themselves when boys are around. And here we had four years to be our goofy, carefree selves. But none of that mattered to me. I was too fixated on the elusive promise of normal, and I thought the only way to get there was to start dating.

With only a few girls from junior high also going to Trinity, I felt lost and nervous in the crowd that first day. I was a trembling, brace-faced, overwaxed, curly-haired teen trying to remember why the hell I had ever taken the test to get into this supposedly prestigious all-girls school in the first place.

I'd set my sights on Trinity because the softball team at the public high school in my town was . . . not good. I knew this because my new stepsister, Jill, went there. My mom had recently gotten remarried to Bobby, a guy she'd gone to high school with. Nicole and I suddenly had a new house and a new blended family. We even had our own bedrooms. Bobby was kind and soft spoken. He was a union tuckpointer with a thick mustache and a big heart. Nicole and I loved Bobby. I knew Jill's school had things like batting cages and a grassy softball field, but all those resources didn't mean that the team won many games. Trinity's softball team didn't have a field and practiced on the asphalt parking lot, but I thought they had potential. And I didn't want to entrust my future, my chance to get into a good college, to a low-ranked softball team at a school that had an average reputation when it came to academics. If I was ever going to get out of Elmwood Park, I needed to take control of my life. Trinity didn't have a stellar reputation or anything, but it was supposed to be a little better than Elmwood Park High, and they bragged that 100 percent of their graduating seniors went on to college. So I'd taken the test to get into Trinity High School, billed as "the Dominican College Preparatory School for Young Women."

One day, sometime right before I exited mass, held in the makeshift church auditorium, to get to third period, my friend Carla grabbed me by the arm to tell me news that would alter my life.

"Do you know Mikey? He thinks you're cute."

He thinks I'm cute? What is this madness you speak of?

Carla had grown up in a town next to Elmwood Park called Melrose Park, and so, too, had this Mikey person. Carla was beautiful and confident, so when she said that her friend, and neighbor, thought I was cute, I paid attention. She opened up her Chandler-branded day planner, the one Trinity had given each of us at the start of the year, and flipped to a page that had a photo pasted on it. I scanned the faces of her friends from elementary school until she pointed Mike out.

Boys like Mike didn't talk to girls like me. He was effortlessly cool and what the girls at Trinity described as "hot." I was . . . not. Boys like him never found girls like me cute. *What was going on?* Sure, I'd dated JP years before, but that was back when the playing field was more even. Back before everyone—except me—got boobs and before everyone—except me—was allowed to shave their legs and armpits. On top of all this, that was before I had taken a trip to the orthodontist. I was no longer just the flat-chested girl with frizzy hair and a mustache; now I was a mostly flat-chested, frizzy-haired, mustachioed girl *with a brace face.* I couldn't quite process what I was hearing. It felt like a tiny miracle was occurring right there in Trinity's makeshift church auditorium. It was as if God Themself were shining down on me.

From the first time I laid eyes on Mikey, I was obsessed with him. Obsessed in every sense of the word. With his impossibly red lips that always looked like he'd just finished sucking on a red lollipop. With his rust-colored eyebrows that were pitched like Boy Scout tents. With the field of dark auburn curls kept at bay by the hairline he inherited from his father. His milk-chocolate eyes were surrounded by thick eyelashes that curled back toward the sky like they were in the upward-facing dog pose. His eyes always looked like they were squinting, just a bit, in the sun.

I don't remember how he asked me out, but I remember mentally sinking into a field of poppies when he did. He made me feel like I was the prettiest girl in the entire world. And when the girls at school found out we were talking, they would gas me up in the hallways, singing: "Mikey and Jen, sitting in a tree—K-I-S-S-I-N-G."

But I wasn't embarrassed. In fact, I was proud. It distracted me from feeling different. It made me feel like one of the girls. And plus, I thought I had found the boy of my dreams.

❦

The first time Mike and I made out, we were watching *Love & Basketball* on his living-room couch. I was cuddled in his arms, and across from us, on the other sofa, his older brother and his older brother's girlfriend were similarly paired. At some point, our lips met each other's for the first time. And like old friends who run into each other at the grocery store, they tried to become awkwardly acquainted. Our teeth clinked, and I worried that my braces had hurt him or, worse, chipped his tooth.

But I instantly loved how it felt to be kissed by Mikey. He tasted so good; I couldn't get enough.

I can't believe this is happening, I thought as he traced my ear with his tongue. His breath gently swirled over the wet, delicate surface, the way wind whips across the tops of skyscrapers.

I love him, I told myself. Just like that, I was falling in love.

A few minutes into that first make-out session, we heard the front door jangling and realized his dad was home.

My heart was pounding so hard, but Mikey remained calm. Unbothered. Like he wasn't raised by a father who reminded you every chance he got that if he caught you with a boy, he'd break that boy's legs and yours. Or maybe that was just what it was like to be raised a son instead of a daughter.

"Hey, Pops, how was work?" he said as his dad wiped his shoes on the doormat and stepped into the house.

"Hey, Mikey. Meh, it was slow," he said in a deep, almost growling voice. He was in his cop uniform, fresh off a shift. He looked tired but in a way that said he was happy to have a job to be tired from.

"Hello, De. Hello, Jen." He gave us a quick wave.

"Hi," we replied in unison. It's all I could manage to squeak out because I was so paranoid that his finely tuned cop senses would pick up the thud of my heart beating.

I realized I felt wet down there, between my legs. I stiffened like a board, and my eyes widened; I was worried that his dad would somehow know. Mikey gently flexed his one-arm embrace of me to tell me that it was okay. I took a deep breath and tried to relax into his arms.

At that exact moment, Mikey secretly squeezed my butt, and my eyes bulged as I tried to hold in a scream.

"You okay?" Mike's dad asked.

"Yeah, just my restless legs syndrome."

Mikey laughed under his breath, his chest moving up and down, and I held my breath until his dad finally said, "Well, all right," and headed up a half landing to the bathroom.

When he was out of view, I jerked my elbow into Mike's rib cage. Wincing a bit and with a smirk across his red, pouty lips, Mikey said, "Calm down, killer, or I'll have my dad arrest you."

It took only a few months for Mike and me to get serious. We both had broken ideas of what real love felt like. Besides making out, fighting was probably the thing we did most.

Our first big fight was at the Spring Fling during my freshman year. The night before the dance, I attended a house party in the basement of a friend's house. The basement was dark and drafty, and in the center of the room was a silver keg. My social life was in a state of purgatory. I had met a few girls at Trinity, but my friend group was still a small mishmash of kids from different schools: a few old friends I'd met in junior high who now went to Trinity with me, some new girls I knew from Trinity, and some old ones who went to the local public high school.

I was going to a new school and was in a phase of mourning for my old friendships. We'd vowed to stay connected, but the separation was insurmountable. The promises we had written to each other in our yearbooks were vows we couldn't keep. When I heard my old friends were throwing a party in the basement, it felt like my last chance to hang out before life forced us apart for good. So I went, by myself, without Mike.

A few hours, some beers, and a bottle of peach schnapps later, I was wasted for the first time. Lying down on the bed in the room where everyone had thrown their coats, I was trying to hold back my vomit. A boy came into the room and sat down on the bed next to me. I knew him from around the neighborhood. He was a year older, but he'd paid me no mind before that night. Suddenly, he was making me feel like I was the prettiest girl in the world—focusing all his attention on me, making me laugh, comforting me as the alcohol turned my stomach. For a second, I forgot about the nausea as he cracked jokes.

Suddenly, he was dragging me into the closet. He shut the door, pushed me down onto the ground by my shoulders, and whipped out his dick. He blocked the door with his husky body and kept one of his hands pressed down on my shoulder while the other attempted to force his dick into my mouth. I was so drunk. I didn't know how I could get out of there. I thought about biting down but was afraid of what he might do if I hurt him, so I froze. I pretended to black out and used all the strength I had to keep my jaw locked shut. Eventually, he gave up and left me in the closet. I waited until I was sure he was gone and then found myself facedown in the toilet bowl, puking and purging the booze, the pain, the memory of what had happened.

I felt disgusted, dirty, and guilty. I was afraid Mikey would blame me, because I blamed myself at the time, and I hoped he would be able to move past the blame stage quickly and comfort me if I was honest and up front.

The entire next day, I felt sick and hungover. If the memory wasn't bad enough, I woke with the puked-up remnants of the night before stuck in my braces. I spent the entire next day with my mother, nauseous in the passenger seat of her pewter Camry as we drove around Chicago, frantically shopping for last-minute corsages, clips for my hair, a powder-blue shawl to go over my shoulders. The nausea stayed with me until minutes before Mike came over. He was dressed up in a button-down and black slacks, and his hair was slicked back with gel.

At that point, my mom had been listening to me gush about Mike for weeks. She was excited to finally put a face to his name, to meet this boy I talked to on the phone each night. Mikey arrived just after eight. He took his shoes off by the door, firmly shook Bobby's hand, and without hesitation boldly kissed my mom on her cheek. It seemed as if the familiar Italian warmth that radiated from his greeting immediately captured the hearts of my Greek-Albanian-Mexican—and now, thanks to my stepdad, Italian-German-Irish—family. As my mother ushered Mike into the kitchen, where the lighting was better for photos, my grandmother pulled me aside.

"So handsome!" she said. "And he took his shoes off!" My family—and my grandmother, in particular—loved his gestures of traditional chivalry. Mike's first impression had left my family swooning.

Mikey and I posed as my mom snapped photos with her yellow-and-black disposable Kodak camera.

At the Spring Fling, Mike's face turned to stone when I confessed about the night before. He stormed out of the gymnasium, throwing one of the cafeteria chairs against the cinder-block wall before leaving me alone at the dance in a puddle of tears.

I should have seen them then, the dynamics both of us were playing out. But I was young and wanted to believe his reaction, his jealousy, just meant he cared. I recognized his temper. It was familiar. His rage felt like my father's, like home.

❦

The week of my sixteenth birthday, Mike and I decided we wanted to have sex. It seemed like every other weekend, another girl at my lunch table had had sex and was spilling the beans to the rest of us virgins as we attentively listened to her tale and ate our Tater Tots. And my varsity softball teammates, many of whom were older than me, were always swapping stories of their hookups at practice. It seemed that everywhere I looked, everyone was getting some. Everyone, that is, except me and maybe the few nuns who roamed the hallways of Trinity.

I was curious. I'd been curious about sex for a long time, ever since I was nine, when I walked in on some of the neighbor boys watching the scrambled Playboy channel in one of their parents' bedrooms.

"What are they doing?" I asked as I crooked my head to the side to try and get a better view.

"Sex," was all they managed to get out, eyes glued to the screen.

The naked woman appeared uncomfortable, like she was in pain.

"But why?" I asked.

"To make babies, duh," one boy replied with a mischievous smile, still unable to look away.

"But . . ."

"Shhhh . . ."

My neighbors were fixated on the spectacle happening before our eyes. I couldn't look away either. I felt the rest of the room fade away as my focus narrowed in on the sex on-screen. I felt the area between my legs—my *vagina*, as my gram taught me it was called—swell. But the area between my legs wasn't the only part of my body whose interest had been piqued. Blood was rushing to my brain as it went into overdrive processing the boy's words: to make babies. *So that's what people do to make babies—babies that I can't make.*

That moment had introduced me to something forbidden that felt titillating, and I was eager to know more. So when my friends' stories about kissing and making out started to be replaced by conversations about sex, I was an eager listener.

Mikey and I planned to have sex on a random night when we knew his dad was working late and his brother was out. We were in Mikey's bedroom, on his bed, making out. My finger fumbled the button of his pants. He was gentle, tender, kind. At one point, he took his shirt off and then took mine off too. The lights were off, and it was dark outside, so I felt comfortable.

I still didn't want anyone to see my body with the lights on.

That feeling I'd had when I'd seen the Playboy channel and made out with Mikey came rushing back—a water balloon filling between my legs, about to burst.

"Are you okay?" he asked. I nodded and said yes. *Oh my God, this is it,* I thought, biting down on my lip and bracing for what was to come. My nerves had been on the moon the entire night, and now they were heading for Mars.

I had read in some women's magazines that your first time is usually painful, and that your cherry popping might cause you to bleed. The girls at school had reported that it wasn't that bad. Some had even said their cherries didn't pop. I hoped I could report back similar findings. I've never been one for pain, even just a bit of it, so I closed my eyes and tried to relax my pelvic muscles like the articles had suggested. I'd read everything the women's magazines and the fledgling internet offered on the subject.

I closed my eyes.

"You okay?" he asked.

"Yes."

The truth was: in that moment, I didn't know what okay was. How does anyone know if they're okay in a new experience? I knew I *wanted* to be okay, and I wanted Mike to *think* I was okay. *Fake it till you make it,* just like Coach Tommy used to yell at me.

But something was wrong. I could feel it. I could see it in his eyes. I stopped trying to relax. It wasn't working anyway. Mike's bare bedroom walls were lit yellow by streetlamps, and his light-blue sheets smelled like Bounce dryer sheets. Vinny, his Jack Russell terrier, was curled up on the floor at the foot of the bed, and a notification light was blinking on Mikey's phone.

Red, green, red, green, red, green.

And then a notification of my own went off: my brain settled on the memory of the moment when the doctor told me, just before my bladder surgery, they'd noticed my vagina was a little bit smaller than those of other girls. They had said they could fix it with a little snip while I was under anesthesia. They had said it would be the only way I could ever have normal sex with my future husband.

After the surgery, during the checkups, the doctors would always peer between my legs and say, *Everything is healing and looks good. No one can tell the difference between you and any other woman.* I'd clung to those words like they were a parachute as I jumped off the cliff of childhood into adolescence. I wanted nothing more in the entire world than for their words to be true.

But I could feel Mike trying to enter me again. And again. And again. My vagina blocked him every time.

"You're . . . really . . . tight," he huffed.

"Thanks?" I said, trying to hold on to my parachute a little bit longer.

I felt shame well up inside, engulfing me. But I fought back the tears and picked a spot just past his face on his bedroom ceiling to focus on. I was trying to dissociate, an astronaut attempting to abandon ship. My vision went blurry as I continued to stare past Mikey until he eventually gave up.

I wasn't just like any other girl. My boyfriend couldn't even fuck me. And I couldn't hold it in anymore. The dam finally broke, and I began crying into his chest. He held me and told me it was okay, that it was going to be okay, but I knew better. Something was wrong.

The doctors were wrong.

A week later, we tried again. And once again, it was a failure. I felt like something awful had been exposed.

A few days after that, we tried a third time.

And as they say, the third time's a charm. I wondered what Mikey must've been thinking. That I was a freak? That I was broken? Did he wonder what was wrong with me? I was just *really tight*, I kept telling myself.

The night we finally had sex was a blur, probably due in part to the copious amounts of alcohol I drank beforehand. I have no concrete memories other than that it happened, and there was pain and some blood. It was so painful that I had to hold my breath and grit my teeth. He asked me if I was okay, like he always had, and I dutifully said yes. But I wasn't.

After six and a half glorious, excruciating minutes, Mike collapsed on top of me. He kissed me. Then he did this thing he knew I loved: sealing my lips with his own and then deeply inhaling before detaching. It made me gasp reflexively for oxygen. He was literally taking my breath away.

When he went to the bathroom, he noticed traces of blood. He walked solemnly back to the bed and lifted the blankets up. There was a small, concentrated pool of blood in the middle of his sheets too. Light-blue fabric soaked and now navy.

"Did I hurt you?" he asked me. His voice was tender and concerned. It was quieter than usual.

"No," I lied.

We left it at that.

It was my cherry, I told myself. *It was just my cherry.*

At school, I didn't mention any of this at the lunchroom table. Instead, I put a smile on my face and shared a carefully crafted narrative that conveniently left out all the embarrassing parts and instead focused on the details that hopefully made me seem just like the rest of my group—a normal girl who was, happily, no longer a virgin.

My first time left me with conflicting emotions. On the one hand, I felt proud that I had finally had sex, that maybe the doctors were right. Maybe I *was* normal. Maybe I was just like every other woman, after all, just with a slightly smaller, tighter vagina. But I also felt confused. It wasn't how I'd imagined it would feel. It had hurt, and I felt so numb afterward. It wasn't how I'd thought it would feel to lose my virginity.

I tried to shrug off that empty feeling. I chalked it up to my inexperience, to being a prude and nervous. I was grasping again at anything that would let me hold on to the narrative that I was like the other girls.

As my high school years slipped by in a haze of drunken parties, uncomfortable sex, and long days on the softball field, Mikey and I became inseparable. We'd make plans to hang out, almost always at Mike's house. We'd watch a movie. And within minutes, making out would lead to sex.

Wash, rinse, repeat.

Eventually the pain I felt in my vagina began to turn into numbness. Just nothing. To this day, I'm not sure which is worse. After the first time we had sex, I didn't think I would ever be able to do it with him again. Going into something not knowing what it would feel like or how badly it would hurt felt exciting and daring. Going into something with the knowledge of what lay ahead was another thing entirely.

But Mikey and I were determined. He was a teenage boy, so of course he wanted to keep trying. I wanted to keep trying because, even after the pain subsided and the numbness took over, I had this unshakable feeling that I had to have sex to be normal. From an early age, I understood in a way that few children do that my worth was intrinsically bound to my ability to have sex. It was as if I could hear Coach Thompson, reminding my teammates for the millionth time: *You gotta go through the motions!* The doctors had pretty much prescribed it. In order to be happy, in order to be loved, I had to have sex with my boyfriend. Then I'd have to marry him. After that, I'd slip in the little tidbit about cancer and not being able to biologically deliver a child, and we'd adopt one instead. Voilà! Life complete.

On top of that, I was also carrying around the feeling of being an inadequate woman, a feeling I'd had ever since I was five and my mom broke the news to me that I wouldn't be able to have children or a period. Every time I let Mike have sex with me, I did so because it allowed me, even if just for a fleeting moment, to feel a little bit more grounded in the fantasy that everything was okay. That I was okay. That I was normal.

But I grew to hate having sex.

After giving up on the hope that one day, with the right position or the right state of mind or the right *whatever*, sex would feel good, I began disassociating every time. Drifting off a little more each time into the exosphere.

When he was inside me and I couldn't feel him anymore, I started to not want to feel me anymore either. I'd go as far away in my mind as I could. Just like when the doctors touched me during appointments. Just like when they put the anesthesia IV in my arm and told me to go to my happy place and count backward from one hundred.

The numbness unfurled across every inch of my body. Every time Mikey came inside of me, which he started doing when I told him my hormone pills were "birth control," a little bit of me browned and curled up like a brittle, dying leaf.

One time after we had just finished having sex on the downstairs sofa, something between my legs caught Mike's eye. He reached behind him and turned on a lamp. He angled its shade just right so he could get a better look, coaxing my thighs apart.

"What are you doing?" I was terrified.

"Getting a better look at you," he said. "Something is different about you."

He examined me with that lamp, the same way the doctors in lab coats had done so many times before. He began probing me until he found a ring of scar tissue between my inner labia, one the doctors must have accidentally made when they were enlarging my vagina—for him.

"I can fit my finger in it," he said.

I wanted to cry and scream and run away, but instead I froze. I'd learned early on, in the days after the surgery, while lying in that hospital bed and during all the checkups that followed, that my body wasn't my own. It didn't belong to me. It belonged to everyone else. It belonged to the people who could "fix" it, to the people who wanted to study it, to the people who would use it.

I froze because I was ashamed of that ring of skin that had hung out of my labia ever since the surgery—I already knew it was there. I already knew something was different. It looked weird, and it rubbed on my panties during the day, often becoming inflamed and painful. I froze because I had no idea what was going on, and no one thought it important enough to give me any tools to help me deal with the transformation of how kissing Mikey went from feeling so good, like I was on cloud nine, to drenching me in a torrent of anxiety about the ensuing sex.

I lay there, vulnerable and paralyzed, crying out to God in my head. *I hate my life. I wish I were dead. Why did you do this to me?*

I lay frozen because I didn't know what else to do, since no one in my life ever had the courage to tell me the complete truth about my body. Being frozen was easier than being thawed and sentient. I felt like prey, and that's what prey does.

By the end of high school, I needed Mikey, and he needed beer. When things were good with us, I was good. When things were bad, my world felt like it was falling apart. Even though I felt dead inside every time we had sex, the alternative—being alone with myself and my painful thoughts—felt worse. I felt like I couldn't live without him. The doctors had hollowed me out, and I craved to be filled back in. I needed him to continue to believe the lie of who I was so I could continue to do the same.

In elementary school, right after my mom broke it to me that I was different—the cancer, no period or babies—a shell began to form around my heart. Then, when my friends started to experience things that I never would, that protective outer layer cracked like one of the scarlet-dyed eggs our family would smash every Greek Easter. With my shell weakened, a noxious lie began to seep in: I wasn't lovable. And before I knew it, the lie that I would have to be perfect to be worthy of love started to feel like a common-sense fact.

Up until puberty, I was doing a decent job—outwardly, at least—of keeping everything intact. Yet when the AP—After Puberty—era of my life began, I felt like I was alone in the middle of a giant theater, strapped to a red velvet seat and forced to watch a play called *Life* in which all the people on stage effortlessly—with no assistance from creepy doctors, shady surgeries, or pills—grew up. My sister was becoming an unavoidable reminder that I wasn't part of the show. Five years younger than me, Nicole was just starting to go through puberty, and I knew the day would come that Kotex and Motrin would appear next to my hormone pill bottles on her side of the medicine cabinet.

I had hoped that going to Trinity with a—mostly—brand-new cast of people in a different town would be the start of a new act. And in some ways, it was. During the fall of my freshman year, I tried out and made the varsity softball team. Thanks to the guidance of Coach Thompson, who still coached me on the weekends and during summer breaks, I was able to help our team climb the ranks. Walking down the hallways on away-game days, when we were given special permission to wear our team uniforms, I felt proud—like I actually belonged. There was nothing better than the warm feeling that would spread across my entire being whenever Sister Michelle, our school's president and our most exuberant fan, crossed my path and gave me a thumbs-up, proclaiming, "Go get 'em, kiddo! Keep making *us* proud!"

Us. The word lingered in the air long after she had said it. It embraced me with a promise of belonging.

When I wasn't playing softball, I started to work. My first job was at a pizza parlor called Amato's across the street from Elmwood Park. When things got busy at the register and on the phones, I often found it difficult to keep track of all that was going on, and invariably, almost nightly, the other staff members and I would have to eat one of my cheesy, melty, delicious mistakes. My manager wasn't happy, but my belly was. And in between all of that, I also managed to hang out with friends and go to school dances and parties on the weekends.

During my junior year, my dreams of playing softball in college on a full ride were seeming less and less like a possibility. At some point during junior high, Coach Thompson decided I'd make a better catcher than an infielder. While I didn't enjoy squatting half of the game and sweating under the clunky catcher's gear, I grew to love the position and got pretty good at it. I was nimble back there, had a good arm for throwing out girls at second base, and lived for those moments when I could launch myself to tag a runner out at home. However, I couldn't help but notice that I stood out against other catchers—and not in a recruitable way. Every single other catcher, even the other one on our team, was solid like a bull, and they were usually the team's cleanup batter because they could hit the living daylights out of the ball. And there I was, the runt who was expected to bunt or slap to get on base.

After I got overlooked by coach after coach, a school finally wrote me a letter of interest and offered to fly me out to visit their campus and meet their players. The school, Rider, was on the East Coast. It felt good to be wanted, and to maybe have a chance at getting that long-hoped-for full ride, but once I got off the plane and arrived on campus, my gut said no. Rider wasn't what I had in mind when I dreamed of college. Instead of a beautiful rolling campus with trees, gray stone buildings, and ivy everywhere, it looked like a beige brick wasteland.

With no better prospects knocking on my door to offer me an athletic scholarship, I slowly and sadly came to the realization that softball wasn't going to be my ticket out. That meant I needed to rely on my grades if I wanted to get out of Elmwood Park and fulfill the dreams of my grandmother, who hoped and prayed I would become a doctor or a lawyer and rise to build a better life. And though my grades were mostly As and Bs, it seemed like every girl at my school had that or better. I feared it wasn't enough for a full ride. I found myself sitting across from my guidance counselor one afternoon during my junior year.

Her office, if you could call it that, was in the tiniest of rooms. Think of a janitor's closet, then think of half of that. Supposedly it used to be a nun's bedroom back when that part of the building was a rectory, but honestly, unless that nun was a small child, I have no idea how she could have lain down and slept in there. It was difficult to even see the counselor behind her clunky monitor and the piles of transcripts and campus brochures stacked on her desk.

"What would you like to major in?" Ms. Pascarella asked before pushing up her oversize glasses, which were like the pair worn by Sophia on *Golden Girls*.

"I don't know." I shrugged. "I used to want to be a veterinarian, but now I don't know anymore."

But I *did* know. I wanted to get recruited by a D-1 team at a school I'd actually heard of. A school that would make my family proud. And then I wanted to play on the Olympic team. And after coming home with a gold medal, I wanted to become a coach and get a deal like Jennie Finch, or one of the other Olympians, who had their own lines of gloves and bats with their signatures printed on them. And then I wanted to get married to Mike and have—*adopt*—babies with him. I didn't have a plan B. I held back tears as the walls of her tiny claustrophobic office closed in.

"Well, have you given any thought to what schools you'd like to apply to? I see you have a twenty-seven on your ACT," she said. "That's pretty good. Could be better but still should give you some options."

I had taken that damn ACT test three different times, and it always came back with the same score: twenty-seven. That number haunted me.

"University of Hawaii?" I asked, even though I was supposed to be giving her an answer.

She cocked her head a bit as if to get a better look at my thoughts. After I rattled off a random list of other schools, threaded together only by the fact that they were all near an ocean and had, I assumed, palm trees nearby, she stopped me.

"Jennifer, do you want to go to a surf school or college?"

I mean, a surf school didn't sound too bad. People who surfed on TV always looked like they were having fun. Maybe softball wasn't my sport. Maybe surfing was and I was just too Midwest to know.

"Before you answer, I need you to get serious about your future," she said. "Take this pamphlet with you, and next time we meet, I want you to have picked five schools from this list that you want to apply to. I'll see you next week."

I let out a sigh as I left her dungeon-size office and filtered my way back into the hallways. I didn't know how to get out of Elmwood Park; a lot of people get comfortable and never leave. I just knew I wanted to be anywhere else but where I was. I wanted to start fresh in a new place without the reminder and memories of my past. It could be softball or surfing or caring for dogs, but I desperately needed something—anything—to whisk me away into a new place, a new life.

After a few months of fretting and stressing, fighting my way through the bureaucracy of the college application process, I ended up applying to a few local, and somewhat local, schools. No Hawaii, no surfboard needed.

When I got my acceptance letter from the University of Illinois, I bounced around the house like a gazelle who'd just escaped the jaws of a predator. I couldn't believe I had gotten in. No one in my family had ever gotten into a four-year university, and there I was, with an acceptance letter to what I had heard was a *really good* school.

"Congratulations, hun," my mom said as she kissed me on my cheek. "I'm so proud of you. I'm so proud of my baby."

I was wrapped in the blanket of her warm words.

"Thanks, Mom," I said, a big smile on my face.

It made me feel fuzzy all over to see my mom be so proud of me.

Then I called my dad. I'd never lived with my dad after he and my mom split up, but while I was in junior high, he'd gotten remarried to a sweet woman named Monika. Monika was born in Poland and moved to Chicago when she was in her late teens. She was a hard worker, a bartender, and had auburn-red hair and big blue eyes. She and my dad had a son named Tommy. A fun-loving boy with round brown eyes and bowl-cut brown hair. Nicole and I spent some of our holidays with them, chowing down on homemade pierogies and other Polish delicacies.

"Hello," he said, sounding defeated. Judging by his tone and the wind in the background, he was driving home from work. A few times a week, he'd drive across state lines in search of good deals on cars at auto auctions. He hated traffic, and it seemed he was always driving in traffic.

"Hey, Dad," I said.

"What's up?" he asked before blurting out, "THIS FUCKING GUY!"

I assumed someone had just cut him off.

"Some prick just cut me off," he said.

My assumption was correct.

"I have some good news!"

"Oh yeah, what is it? I need some good news because the auction was shit today," he said.

"I got into U of I!" I said with equal dashes of excitement and trepidation.

"Congratulations, baby!" he said.

I could imagine his smile. He was genuinely happy for me. I could hear it even through all the noise.

"I'm so proud of you. Oh man, that's great. Really great. Oh, I'm so proud of you, baby!"

I basked in my parent's adulation.

"I can't wait till you graduate and buy your old man an island so I don't gotta be stuck in this traffic no more!" he said as the blaring honk of a semi's horn trailed off in the distance.

Whenever my dad expressed tiny wishes for a different sort of life, I felt sad. Getting accepted to a university with a good reputation, like U of I, was an opportunity to help out not only my future self but also my parents. Money, and the stress that came from never having enough of it, was like gravity—ever present and seemingly impossible to change. I was at a precipice looking across at the other side, legs trembling, hoping I could stick the landing—or at least climb back up if I fell. And when I made it to the other side, I tucked a quiet prayer in my heart. A prayer that asked for the ability to one day help relieve my parents' financial stress. Sometimes I caught glimpses of my dad on that island he talked about, and of my mom just finally relaxing instead of working all day and night. When I envisioned my parents like this, I could feel my body relax as if every pore exhaled.

While my parents seemed mostly happy about my acceptance to the big state school—I say *mostly* because tensions were already beginning to boil over the loans that we'd have to take out to cover the costs—one person was definitely not happy: Mike.

As the summer waned, I began to doubt my decision to go. Mikey was certain that distance, a couple of hours' drive south, would not make us grow fonder—it would lead to us breaking up. He made it clear that if I chose to leave for school instead of going to a closer college, I was essentially choosing to end our relationship. I didn't want to see it that way.

I wanted to believe that we could endure the distance, taking turns on weekends to travel to see each other. And I didn't feel like I was able to take the leap to this next chapter of my life without him. Yeah, our relationship checked off most, if not all, of the trademarks of a toxic relationship, but I didn't yet understand all that. And like most relationships, there wasn't only the bad; there was also the good. He was my first real love, and I felt like I needed to be with him. I couldn't stand the idea of losing him. I had spent the past four years of high school weaving my sense of self-worth with his sense of desire for me. Like the tides of the ocean, waxing and waning under the tug of the moon, my well-being was tethered to the status of our relationship. That lie—that I needed a relationship to make me whole, as my doctors had all but prescribed—was why the decision to go away to college and possibly destroy my relationship with Mikey was gnawing away at every fiber of my being.

Mikey wasn't perfect. He had a temper that scared me, and his affinity for alcohol got worse as the years went on. We'd get into intense arguments, which sometimes got physical, and it often seemed we spent more time fighting than not. There were even a few times when he cheated on me. But I lived for those moments with my head lying on his chest, listening to the beat of his heart as he'd kiss me on the crown of my head and whisper, "I love you." We were two kids in pain, unsure of what love was but trying to numb ourselves and pretend otherwise.

And what mattered most was that Mike didn't seem to notice I wasn't quite right. It took him a while to catch on to my hormone pills, which I kept stashed in my sock drawer, and when he finally did, I just told him it was birth control the doctors prescribed to me because I had to have my cancerous ovaries removed when I was a baby. He bought it. He also seemed to believe me when I lied and said I was on my period, which I sometimes tried to sell by painfully shoving a tampon up inside of me as a prop. I had hoped that the visual of the tampon's braided cotton string would convince Mikey that I was, indeed, like every other girl who bled once a month.

When I imagined my future, I imagined it with Mikey. I was convinced that we were in love, and perhaps equally as important, I was afraid anyone else would be able to tell that I'd had surgery down there. That I wasn't normal. Mikey hadn't realized how abnormal I really was, and anyone else, I was certain, would come to the conclusion that I was a freak.

He allowed me to hide. I wanted to marry Mike and have a family with him when I got out of college. The fear of losing Mikey—and in a sense my ability to pass as normal—to the world and to myself—led me to turn down my dream school. I stayed with Mikey and went to DePaul, a smaller Catholic school in the city. I just couldn't risk letting go of what I'd built; I was willing to sacrifice to make myself feel safe.

PART II

CHAPTER 6

And then the moment came when my life's compass shattered, when a portal opened up in the multiverse.

I was sitting in the back of a cramped and dimly lit classroom at DePaul University. My professor, Jessica, a tall, gentle, pale-skinned woman, paced in front of the whiteboard in her pantsuit and her Ann Taylor pumps. Just before we were about to break, she put up a slide that read "Androgen Insensitivity Syndrome."

Say it five times fast.

Go ahead.

I'll wait.

Or you can just call it AIS.

The class was Psychology of Women 300. One of my high school teachers—Ms. Bocio—had introduced me to theories of psychology and feminism in a fun and creative way. So when I saw Jessica's course on the list of available classes, it leaped out. After all, I identified as a woman and wanted to know more about who I was and how the psychology of my mind worked.

We met every Tuesday and Thursday for an hour. I wasn't supposed to be there. It was my freshman year, and I had applied without quite knowing what the "300" meant. Turns out, it's kind of an important detail—the 300-level psych courses are usually reserved for upper-level students with years of psychology under their belts. How was I supposed to know? There was one other freshman in the class, too, and they were just as clueless as I was.

"How old are you, anyway?" my adviser asked, looking at a list of courses I'd already signed up for.

"Eighteen?" I answered, like I was unsure.

"Jen, for Pete's sake, this class isn't usually taken by freshmen!"

And yet there I was. I was wearing my Ugg boots, a black North Face fleece, and this sparkly purple eyeshadow I'd stolen from Target. (It was 2005; what do you expect?) I looked the part of a bubbly first-year student in a small classroom of twenty, and the lecture was absolutely decimating my reality.

Given the circumstances, however, I thought I was having a rather polite nervous breakdown. The girl to my left had her head down, headphones blasting, listening to Evanescence, completely unaware my life had just irrevocably changed.

Now, AIS—like all intersex variations—is super complex, but I'll try to give you the lowdown the best I can. Buckle in!

For the first six weeks of development in the womb, embryos are sexually indifferent. Regardless of sex chromosomes—the twenty-third pair responsible for a person's sex characteristics—their gonads, internal reproductive tracts, and external genitalia are identical. After week six, embryos typically begin to sexually differentiate, starting first with the gonads. All gonads can form into either testes or ovaries, and that development is dictated by sex chromosomes, which hold the blueprints, so to speak. If the chromosomal sex is XY, then usually the gonads will become testes, and their internal and external genitalia will masculinize—and vice versa if the chromosomal sex is XX.

I said *typically* and *usually* while describing this process because, as I found out that day in my class, it's not always what happens. Sometimes an embryo rebels. Enter androgen insensitivity syndrome, or AIS.

When a person is born with AIS, their sex chromosomes are XY—the typical chromosomes for babies who are assigned male at birth. But AIS infants are usually assigned female at birth because their external genitalia appear feminine. However, a pair of unde-scended testes (instead of ovaries) and a *blind-ending* vagina that doesn't lead to a cervix or uterus are present. The AIS body is able to convert androgens—hormones, such as testosterone, that are respon-sible for the development of male sex characteristics—into estrogens, or hormones that are responsible for the development of female sex characteristics. This magic trick of sorts is partially able to occur because androgens, as it turns out, are precursors to estrogens.

So let's say you're an AIS baby and your little undescended baby balls start making testosterone, right? A person with AIS would be, like, *Nah, I'm good.* Their body would not respond to the testosterone. Instead, it would say, *Abracadabra*, and—poof!—it would convert the testosterone into estrogen. And since an AIS person's genitalia started in a sex-neutral state, like all embryos, and their body isn't responding to androgens, instead converting them to estrogens, which it can respond to, an XY AIS infant is often born looking virtually indistinguishable from XX female infants.

To make matters a bit more complicated, AIS is an umbrella cat-egory for two subdiagnoses: complete androgen insensitivity (CAIS) and partial androgen insensitivity (PAIS). PAIS is just like CAIS, except there is only a partial insensitivity to androgens, and thus, PAIS babies usually come out of the womb with genitalia that has more ambiguity than their CAIS counterparts. The PAIS embryo almost masculinizes but doesn't quite do so completely, so the infant is often born with genitalia that is visibly neither completely feminine nor completely mas-culine in appearance. Genital sex traits like swollen labia, partially fused labia, bifurcated scrotums, enlarged clitorises, and/or different degrees of hypospadias—a term that describes when the urethra doesn't open at the tip of a penis/phallus—can all be apparent in PAIS individuals. Because PAIS traits aren't hidden from plain view like those of CAIS, which often goes undiagnosed for years, an individual with PAIS is usually diagnosed at birth or very soon after.

Now that you have a primer in AIS and sexual dimorphism in humans, I'd like to go back to when I was eighteen years old and sitting in my women's psych class, moments before I cracked for the first time.

The slide listed other facts about people with AIS too—facts that curiously seemed to describe me:

. . . can't have children . . .

Check.

. . . unable to have a period . . .

Check.

These were two things I had known about myself since I was five years old. But I'd been told it was because I was born with cancer in my ovaries—not because I had AIS.

I was told the doctors had performed a dangerous ovary removal surgery on me before I was a year old to save my life. I was told the surgery they performed on me at ten was to keep my bladder functioning properly. And the little add-on vaginal enlargement procedure was nothing special, just something to make me more comfortable once I was married. They said it was the only way I could have sex with my future husband.

Then my professor clicked to a new slide:

"Women with AIS have XY chromosomes," she said.

Wait a minute, I thought. *XY is the chromosome makeup for boys.* That didn't make any sense, because I was a girl. My birth certificate said so. I was still in a relationship with my boyfriend, coming up on five years. I had played for a traveling girls' softball team and had graduated from an all-girls Catholic high school. If I had XY chromosomes, there's no way those Catholic nuns would have let me in.

But there were those two letters staring back at me.

XY.

I felt my chest begin to tighten. It seemed like I was breathing through a pinched straw, like I was the only one in the classroom as everyone else faded away. I was in one of those weird-ass surrealist Dalí paintings, where the clocks start to do whatever they're doing. I couldn't breathe. I couldn't scream.

It was all a lie? Everyone had been lying to me my entire life?

During the mid-lecture break, I raced back to my room clutching my notebook. I rushed into my cinder-block dorm and locked the solid wood door behind me. My roommate was out, at the quad or in class. I didn't know, but I was grateful she wasn't around. I sat down and opened my notebook at my desk. My mind was racing. My gut already knew the truth, but I decided to call my mom anyway.

"How are you?" Her tone was casual.

"I'm good," I said, trying not to explode. "How are you?"

"I'm good," she said. "Exhausted but good. How are classes going?"

"They're okay," I said. "That psychology class is hard, but Mom, I have a question for you. I was in class today, and the teacher was talking about something. And I know you said last time we talked that you just got some of my documents from the hospital in the mail. I need to know what they say. I need to know if they say anything about a diagnosis."

"Okay, sure, hun, hold on a sec," she said. "That reminds me, we have to schedule a gynecology appointment for you . . ."

When I turned eighteen, Children's Memorial Hospital, since renamed Lurie Children's Hospital, had sent my mom paperwork so we could start transitioning me from pediatric care to seeing a gynecologist who treated adults.

"Okay, I found it," she said. "The envelope was in my drawer!"

My mom kept everything important in that goddamn sock drawer. I do the same thing in mine.

"What does it say?" I asked.

"Hold on, let me look. Okay, it says . . . yada yada yada . . . diagnosis! Found it. Andro . . . gen insensi . . ."

I threw my flip phone against the wall of my dorm room, smashing it into pieces.

As I looked into the mirror, my reflection was blurred by the tears that burned my eyes. I studied my features and felt total shock over all the things I hadn't really acknowledged, or wasn't able to realize, before that moment. Things were seemingly becoming clearer. It was like I was finally able to see one of those Magic Eye optical illusions—evidence hidden in plain sight.

But evidence of what? A giant human question mark stared back at me. It had breasts, arched eyebrows, wavy chestnut hair, fake diamond stud earrings, a teal hoodie, high-set cheekbones, no beard but definitely a Frida mustache.

I'm a guy? I'm a fucking guy. I can't believe this. No. No. No. This can't be . . . No. I can't believe they've been lying to me since I was five. Who lies to their kid like that? How is this really my life?

Then I started thinking about all of the doctors' visits, my pee problem, the bladder surgery—*We're just going to make your vagina a little bit bigger*—the doctor's instructions to keep my hormones and lack of a period private. *Nobody needs to know.* All the interns and doctors spreading my legs to view my privates. The way sex with Mike just always seemed not quite right. And then there was that other thing, the thing about myself that I was most ashamed of, the fact that ever since I had started masturbating, my natural inclination was to lie down on my chest and hump a pillow—*like a boy.* I had never told a single soul about it, and I'd carried so much shame.

I couldn't dwell on my pillow-humping crisis for too long because another concern popped into my head.

A queasy weight plopped down at the bottom of my stomach.

What about Mikey? How was I going to tell my boyfriend that I was a guy?

I had successfully staved off the demise of our relationship by choosing a school in the city over one far away in the cornfields. Regardless of our physical proximity, we were developing an emotional distance that was getting harder to ignore. Ever since I'd started college, I'd begun building memories that Mike felt left out of—compounding our existing problems. I'd begun meeting new people. These new people mostly lived in the same dorm but were unlike anyone else I had met before. They were into bands like Led Zeppelin and Dashboard Confessional; they watched artsy films with actors and directors I had never heard of; and weirdest of all, they liked to buy used clothes from thrift stores. I'd finally started to feel like I was fitting in with these kids. It was these new friends who had introduced me to the joy of smoking weed while listening to "Stairway to Heaven" and talking about the wonders of the universe. It was an experience unlike any I'd had before that. In high school, I'd smoked weed to not feel things. In college, it was the opposite. It was helping me to feel and realize things.

After I took off for college, so, too, did many of Mike's friends. He chose work over school, and his schedule had thrust him into an adulthood that made him feel left out, a loneliness he sometimes tried to soothe with cheap beer.

College was expanding the way I felt about myself, but I wasn't ready to let go of Mikey. And as soon as I confirmed that I had AIS, I started worrying that, when Mike found out, he'd be outraged. It was one thing to hide ovarian cancer and barrenness, but now I knew that I had XY chromosomes, that I was technically *a boy*, and that felt different. I was terrified Mike would feel duped, as if I had been lying to him this entire time—whether I meant to or not—and I feared he would hurt me, or himself, in a fit of rage.

❦

A few days after I got the news that shattered my world, I woke up numb. My mind was swirling with disbelief. *Was it a dream?* I had another psychology of women class, so I dragged myself out of bed. I was running on fumes. No sleep, no appetite. I had cried every day since our last class, and my face was swollen and red. I felt depleted and dehydrated and completely detached from my body, from my life. But something was propelling me forward. I needed to talk to somebody about what I'd found out. I threw on my already worn clothes and dragged myself to class. I was both eager and dreading this opportunity. As the ninety-minute-long lecture ended, I waited for the class to clear out and then approached my professor, Jessica.

"Can you talk for a sec?"

"Sure." She nodded.

It took me a moment to figure out exactly what to say. It felt impossible to claim the things I'd been living with in my head. "I think I have that thing," I shyly managed to say to her.

She tilted her head a bit to the side, the way a puppy does.

"What thing?" She looked concerned.

"That thing you were talking about in class the other day. AIS."

Just saying the letters out loud caused me to burst into tears. I was getting good at crying.

I told Jessica everything I knew. I told her how I hadn't been sleeping. Hadn't done any homework for her or any other class. I told her how AIS had completely taken over my life.

"They lied to me," I said, sobbing.

"Oh, sweetheart, I'm so sorry," she said. "I'm so, so sorry."

I could tell she meant it.

"Next week we have a speaker coming to our class. She's from ISNA's speakers bureau. ISNA is the Intersex Society of North America. If you'd like, I can arrange for us three to get pizza together. Would that be okay?"

"Yeah, okay," I said. "I would like that. Thank you."

But again, I was saying whatever I thought I should say. The truth was, I wasn't sure if I would like that. I didn't want to be rude. I'm midwestern.

"Okay, I'll set it up. And I'm here if you need anything," Jessica said warmly.

"Okay, thank you," I replied, unsure of what her offer really meant. What I really wanted was for my mother to hold me and tell me this was all just a bad dream. Or for my father to say he'd never let them hurt his baby girl, that none of this had happened. I wanted Mike to swoop in and tell me I was going to wake up soon. But every path to safety led to a dead end. I felt I couldn't turn to those I loved and trusted the most. I didn't have anyone to turn to, and I felt so alone.

And what about my new friends? As much as we had a blast hanging out with one another, the truth is, I wasn't comfortable facing my new social circle with this revelation. I immediately felt the familiar need to hide my new reality from everyone around me.

❦

The days after I found out the truth were a blur. I had fallen down an internet rabbit hole and done a gazillion hours of research on AIS. I had no desire to sleep or eat for days because the research took precedence over every other need. My deep descent into an internet intersex wormhole was a hyperfocused frenzy of need. The world around me seemed to melt away as I consumed every ounce of research that I could hunt down. If there was something uploaded to the web about AIS, I had read it.

The rest of the week passed in that haze of isolation. With no working phone to break up the aloneness, I sank further into a hole of despair until the day finally came. The day that I was going to be in the same room, knowingly, with someone like me, whatever that meant.

Students shuffled into class and were chatting with each other as they sat down. I usually sat in the middle-front of the class, but that day I took a seat in the back row, my back against the wall. Jessica was at the front of the room facing us, getting her PowerPoint set up on the computer. She and the guest speaker, Lynnell, had walked in together, and it seemed that they were friendly, judging by their banter. I glanced at Lynnell. Looking at her felt a bit like seeing myself for the first time.

She was wearing an oversize denim button-up with the sleeves rolled up. Tattoos peeked out beneath her cuffs. Her chinos and leather boots finished off the outfit, and her hair was twisted in shoulder-length microlocs. She had an eyebrow piercing and another silver ball below the center of her bottom lip. When she laughed, which she did often during her private conversation with Jessica, huge dimples appeared in her golden-brown cheeks. She had an air of confidence about her that was impossible not to pick up on. Apparently, we didn't have everything in common.

Butterflies raced in my stomach as I waited for her to begin her presentation.

"All right, class," Jessica began, "today I'm so honored to introduce our guest speaker, Lynnell Stephani Long. Lynnell is a member of the Intersex Society of North America's speakers bureau and a longtime intersex advocate and activist."

She turned to Lynnell and said, "Without further ado, please welcome Lynnell."

The class perked up a bit and focused their attention on the new person at the front who was serving us leather-daddy butch vibes.

"Thank you, Jessica," Lynnell said through a smile that lit up her entire face.

"As Jessica said, I'm Lynnell. I'm with ISNA. And today I'm going to talk to you all about intersex."

She had the slightest lisp, which I found absolutely endearing.

Lynnell stood in front of us and bared her soul about her childhood. She was incorrectly assigned male at birth by doctors and was raised to believe she was a boy. Yet she never masculinized like the other boys and thus stood out. She became a target for their bullying and harassment. On top of that, for reasons unbeknownst to Lynnell at the time, her mom started dropping her off at the University of Chicago's Children's Hospital for entire summers. There the doctors experimented on her with novel hormone treatments that made her very sick, and not in the very least any more masculine appearing.

"I was raised by a single Black mother on the South Side, and the doctors took advantage of her, of us," she said. "They told my mom they were going to help her baby boy for free."

At some point during Lynell's recounting of her childhood story, the dam inside me broke, and tears began flooding from my eyes. Lynnell was able to crack jokes and make everyone laugh. Even me, with my snotty, teary-eyed wreck of a self. But her story was still one of the most tragic things I had ever heard. I couldn't handle the pain I felt for her. For me. For us.

Class came to an end, and everyone except Jessica, Lynnell, and me shuffled out of the classroom.

"You still able to join us for pizza, Jen?" my professor asked, tenderly.

I nodded.

Walking as far behind them as I could, I followed Lynnell and Jessica to the pizza place across the street from campus. I was so insecure at the time, so afraid of others finding out this newfound truth about me. I thought that if I was seen walking with my professor and our intersex guest speaker, then everyone on campus would be able to see me, the real me, and I wasn't able to cope with that. Not yet. So instead, I was out there walking three yards behind them, like a creepy shadow, with my eyes glued to the ground. Toddler logic set in, and I thought that just maybe if I didn't see anyone, they wouldn't see me.

When we finally made it the few blocks to the pizza place, I couldn't keep my distance anymore. The host asked us how many, and Lynnell replied, "Three, please." Standing there, one of our party of three, I was the closest I had ever knowingly been to another intersex person. The hours I had spent reading about AIS online alone in my dorm the past few weeks had led to me finding and joining a private Yahoo! Group for women with AIS and reading *all* their stories. Those stories were all tightly packed into one never-ending Microsoft Word document that I was given access to once I had finally been admitted to the group. My story, which was a requirement for entrance into the support group, had been added, tacked on at the very end of the document because I was the newest member. As I read, our stories all blended together. We had all been lied to in similar ways. We were all dealing with the same kind of stigma and shame. Most of us were scared and hiding in the anonymous comfort of an online group.

But not Lynnell.

Lynnell wore her PAIS with pride, like it was just another one of her tattoos. She was loud and proud to be a dyke, and she was proud of being intersex. Every other word out of her mouth was *intersex* this and *lesbian* that. To be honest, it made me uncomfortable. Couldn't she just tone it down a bit? Why did she have to walk around and be so *intersex*? Why couldn't she just be normal? I was beginning to regret my decision to come.

I started looking around the room for possible escape routes. How could I get out of this place unseen and unscathed by my association with these people? I glanced to my left, then to my right, and didn't see anyone I recognized. After realizing Lynnell was looking right at me as I cased the joint, I smiled and buried my gaze in the menu.

"Do you know what you want?" Lynnell asked me. "Because I'm starving."

"Ummm, yeah, I'll get the gnocchi with vodka sauce," I replied. Gnocchi felt safe. Mike's mom had introduced me to the immeasurable joys of pillowy gnocchi with vodka sauce; it was my favorite Italian dish—and a connection back to when things were simpler.

"Lynnell, you were great today," Jessica said. "Thank you so much for coming to speak. I think the students really got a lot out of it."

"Thank you," Lynnell said with a grin. "What about you?" she asked me. "Did you like it? I saw you were crying."

I nodded.

"Oh, yeah, it was great. I liked it. You're really funny. It was just, you know, a lot."

I let out another deep exhale.

"Jessica tells me you have AIS too? And that the hospital you went to is nearby?"

"Yeah, I do," I said, feeling the weight of the words in my mouth. "I just found out in her class a few weeks ago."

"And what hospital did you go to?"

"Children's, right over there," I said, pointing with my eyebrows.

"Children's Memorial?" she asked.

"Yup."

"Have you gotten your medical records yet?" she asked.

"No," I replied.

"You got to try and get them. Especially since it's right across the street. You can walk there! Not many intersex people have been able to retrieve their records. Everyone's seemed to have *burned in a fire*," she said while making air quotes. "When you go, just tell them you want a copy, and don't let your doctors know you're requesting them. It'll cost money that way, but it's better to pay for them so your doctors don't have a chance to cover anything up."

I listened intently to Lynnell's instructions. She was imparting intersex wisdom that, I would later learn, was passed down from intersex generation to generation.

"How much do you think it'll cost?" I asked, thinking about the seventeen dollars in my bank account.

"It shouldn't be too much, maybe a quarter a page," Jessica chimed in. That didn't seem too bad. But then Lynnell's eyes narrowed and her forehead furrowed. She leaned in close.

"Have you said that you're intersex out loud yet?" Lynnell asked me.

"Huh?" I said, stunned.

"Have you said you're intersex?" Lynnell repeated, more slowly this time.

"No," I said suspiciously.

Why would I do that? I'm a normal girl. I don't want to be a freak.

"You need to," she said. "You need to say it. You need to say, 'I'm intersex.'"

I stared at her.

At this point, I was pretty sure this bitch was crazy.

"Go ahead, say it," Lynnell said.

"I'm intersex," I said, my voice barely audible.

"Say it louder, say it prouder!" she urged.

"I'm intersex," I said, a scant decibel louder this time.

"Louder!"

"I'm intersex . . ."

"Louder!"

"I'm intersex . . ." The volume increased each time, and I started to forget where I was, what I was risking.

"I'm intersex."

I'm intersex!

CHAPTER 7

I stood at the counter of Lurie's medical record office, which was tucked below the main lobby in the basement of the aging building. I was chewing my fingernails as my medical records came spitting out of the Xerox machine, too hot to touch. The stack of papers must've weighed fifteen pounds.

Walking back to my dorm room, I held in my hands the answer to a question that had plagued me every minute since my mom uttered "androgen insensitivity syndrome" on the phone: What did those doctors do to me? Guilty bubbles rose to the surface containing pockets of hope that what I was about to read wouldn't be as bad as what had happened to Lynnell and some of the others in the support group. Maybe, just maybe, I had been spared. The experience I was about to embark on—locking myself in a suffocating cinder-block room and finally reading the truth—was shattering and felt absolutely singular. At that point in time, there was no road map for going through this. There was no precedent for it. No counselors were equipped to help. There were no safe spaces where I could turn. There was no LGBTQIA+ resource center like there is today. I was in uncharted waters here.

I held the pages close to my body, feeling as if I had to hide them so nobody would know. I tried to muster up the strength to read them, but I couldn't. Something was stopping me. As strong as I wanted to be, I felt I needed support. And I only knew one person I could call: Lynnell.

I was at a table by myself in a small study hall room. I dialed Lynnell's number on my cell and waited for her to answer.

"Lynnell? I'm sorry to bother you. I need to talk and—"

"You're not bothering me," she said, interrupting my apology. "I told you you could always call me. And I meant it."

I told her I was holding my medical records in my hands and needed somebody to be with me. I needed her support as I read through them for the first time. I could tell she understood. It felt as if she'd been expecting this call.

"Wow, so yours weren't burned in a fire like the rest of ours," she said with a whip of sarcasm aimed at every hospital that told a fellow patient this lie about their records. I guessed I was lucky that I'd at least know what they did. *Lucky* felt like the wrong word, though.

I shook as I began to page through them. I scanned the documents, and my eyes flared with terror, fury, fear, and despair. The first page I saw read: "46 XY male pseudo-hermaphrodite."

I started flipping through, and other things caught my eye:

". . . the gonads were abnormal . . ."

". . . clitoral enlargement was 1.5 centimeters . . ."

". . . testicular feminization . . ."

". . . vaginoplasty . . ."

". . . the chromosomes are XY . . ."

". . . androgen insensitivity syndrome . . ."

Pages of doctors' notes about how they removed my undescended testes. Others detailing genital surgeries that left me with tons of scar tissue and nerve damage. I thought back to Mike and the numbness I felt when we'd try to have sex. The pain I felt. The shame I felt. His words: *Something is different about you.* And now it all began to make sense.

There was something else that didn't make it into these documents: I never had cancer.

I wasn't born with cancerous ovaries. I didn't have ovaries at all. Instead, my records confirmed I was born with undescended testes, or *streak gonads*, as they were sometimes described, and the doctors had told my parents that if they weren't immediately removed, these gonads would be cancerous by the time I hit puberty. On one page, there was a note mentioning that while the doctors were in a meeting with my parents, they only used the word *gonads*, not *testes*. They did everything they could to render the parts of me that weren't feminine—those parts incongruous with their decision that I should be raised a girl—null.

But the cancer risk they had warned my parents about was way overinflated. It was a scare tactic they often used to persuade frightened parents. And instead of advising parents like mine to tell their kids the truth, the doctors told them to tell us we were born with cancerous ovaries that had to be removed in order to save our lives. This way, the scars and lack of menses made sense, and the story—that we were normal girls who just happened to be born with cancer in our reproductive parts—could persist.

It felt like I had been kicked in the stomach. My entire life was becoming a sex-and-gender *Truman Show*—constructed for me by people who thought they knew better.

I could see it all so clearly now. The narrative the doctors had crafted for my parents was that I was an underdeveloped female child. All the procedures they convinced my parents to consent to would help me *fully* develop. None of the surgeries were about preserving my health—they were all purely cosmetic.

The system didn't want to say that I'm intersex. That I'm not female or male. The doctors wanted to choose a gender for me and then make my body agree with their ideas about who I should be.

I sat there with my face in my hands. And after hours on the ground paging through my entire medical history, there was only one thing not included in those pages: my voice. My voice was absent from the entire stack of medical records. Not once did anybody ever ask me what I wanted for myself.

My chromosomes chose intersex.

My doctors chose girl.

And I was left to endure the consequences.

❧

Weeks had passed, and I had to come to a point in my life I had been avoiding. I needed to call my mother back and ask her what happened. I needed to know why.

I had started going back to classes, reacclimating myself to college life. Once again, I fell back on my old coach's mantra: *Fake it till you make it.* But this time there was no making it. Make it to what? To a place where I was a mutant whom no one, not even myself, understood? Forget that; I wanted to be normal. I wanted that normal college experience. So instead, I just tried my best to put on a smile and act like nothing had happened. I still hadn't had a conversation with Mike or told anyone else in my life, except Lynnell and those in the online support group, about what I had learned. And I wasn't about to tell anyone. I was terrified. But I knew I needed to talk to my mom. And I knew she wanted to talk too. My voice mail was filled with messages from her pleading to talk with me.

After smashing my phone to pieces, I had disappeared. I hadn't answered her calls. I knew my mother was worried, but I was still too angry to talk. I didn't know what to say. On some level, I knew if I reached out and asked my mom to meet up, she would. Or I could've hopped on the bus and gone home to hash things out. But I was beyond angry. I was unreachable. Unreasonable and furious. I felt in control for the first time in my life. I was the one calling the shots now; I had spent my entire life having other people make irresponsible decisions for me regarding my body. And suddenly I was supposed to be the bigger person and reach out? What could she possibly say, anyway? What words could she say that would heal the scars?

Weeks of silence went on between us. But grieving alone in my dorm room, so far away from my family, began to take its toll on me. I eventually realized I couldn't get through this alone. I needed my mother. I wanted to curl up in her lap and have her slowly tickle my back, like she did when I was little, and tell me everything was going to be okay. That's when I dialed her number.

"Mom?" I said sheepishly.

"Jen? Jen! Hi, hun!" she exclaimed into the phone.

She sounded so relieved.

I immediately started crying, our last conversation playing in my head. I felt guilty.

"I'm sorry I haven't called you, but I broke my phone after we talked last time, and . . ."

"Are you okay?"

"Yeah, I'm okay, Mom," I said into the receiver. "I'm fine."

"My God, I've been worried sick about you!" she said. "I was about to come down there after work tomorrow to make sure you were okay."

"I'm coming home this weekend," I said. "We need to talk."

"I'll make tacos," she said.

Her tacos were my favorite. She deep-fried the corn tortillas in hot grease, like her grandmother had done when she was a kid, which made them delicious and highly addictive.

"Okay, Mom. I'll see you Saturday." We hadn't said much, but at least we'd broken the silence.

❀❀✖❀❀

That weekend, I packed an overnight bag and walked over to Fullerton to wait at the bus stop. Once the 74 bus arrived, I stepped on, swiped my bus card, and took a seat like I'd done so many times before. With my head leaning on the giant window, I watched the campus disappear as we headed west and tried to brace myself for what was waiting for me at home.

The bus from DePaul down to my mother's house in Elmwood Park takes about forty minutes. During one of the stops, I saw a pigeon dance their way on.

I had always hated pigeons.

I guess I hated them because everybody else seemed to. For many, the pigeon was not really a bird but more of a rat with wings. A hideous pest that infiltrated our pristine public spaces, determined to poop on all our heads and defile the bronze heads of park statues.

But there was something different about the pigeon that came onto the bus that day. Or maybe I was the one who was different. Either way, I sat there on the bus smiling at this bird I used to find grotesque. There was something beautiful about this pigeon and the way it had decided to get on the bus and give its wings a break. I could've cried. I watched as they walked up and down the blue vinyl grooves of the bus's center aisle, bobbing their head back and forth as they went. This pigeon acted as if their behavior were standard. They acted as if they were a commuter, too, and riding the bus was something they did every now and then, when they were too tired to fly. Maybe *we* were the weird ones for looking at them the way we did. Maybe *we* were the ones who were strange for caring so much about a bird taking the bus.

When I finally got home, Coco, our big yellow lab mix, was standing at the door with her pink-and-brown nose smushed against the glass as her tail wagged. I was happy to see her too.

I turned the door latch and let myself in.

The air in the kitchen was thick and smelled like garlic and ground beef. My gram, who was coming down the stairs from her bedroom on the second floor, was the first to see me. She immediately cracked a smile.

"Look who finally came home to see ussssss."

"Hi, Gram," I said, blushing.

Then I put my backpack down on the floor before giving her a big hug and a kiss on the cheek. She had on a pair of teal joggers and a matching crewneck sweatshirt, and she smelled like her Issey Miyake perfume. Her nails were orangey-pink-red and looked like she had just gotten them done.

My mom hollered from the kitchen.

"Jen, hun, is that you?"

I picked up my backpack before walking into the kitchen to greet my mom. I gave her a hug and a kiss on the cheek.

"Hi, Mom," I said.

"Hi, hun!" she said before turning to continue stirring the meat.

I hated initiating conversations. The anticipation of having to start this one had kept me up all night tossing and turning, and had made my stomach hurt on the bus ride home. *The longer I wait, the longer I'll feel this way*, I thought.

I needed to get it over with.

"Mom," I said.

"Yeah, hun?" she said with her back still turned to me as she shredded a brick of cheese.

"Can you stop for a minute and sit down?"

She put the half brick of cheese down and grabbed a glass lid to cover the meat before lowering the flame. Then she took a seat at the kitchen table. I sat down, too, and took a deep breath.

I spoke slowly. I explained to her everything I had learned. I told her the doctors had cut off my clitoris, and I described the specifics of androgen insensitivity. I still wasn't comfortable talking about this type of stuff with my mother, despite all we'd been through, but I knew I had to be specific to see what she knew and to make clear everything that had been done to me. While she knew the surgeries had taken place, she didn't seem to know the toll they had taken on my body. She didn't seem to know the extent to which they had harmed me.

My mother paused. She looked like she was taking it all in. Deep, deep in thought. I felt like we were making progress. She was listening to me, and we were going to figure this out together.

"You still get turned on by boys, though, right, hun?"

"What?" I asked her.

I was incredulous. I couldn't believe what I had just heard. I had just opened my heart to my mom about the maltreatment I had experienced at the hands of my doctors. I had just tried to lay out for her all of the things I had learned about my body and what was done to it. I was feeling extremely sensitive and vulnerable, and that was her first question?

"Seriously?" I snapped.

I was enraged. I needed answers and comfort. I needed her to know what they had put me through and to acknowledge that something had been stolen from me.

"Yeah," she said. "Do you still want to date boys?"

My mother, I decided, was still in denial. It felt as if she couldn't bring herself to fully face what had happened to me. And, like most people of her generation, she had been inundated with homophobia her entire life. Maybe she was worried about how hard my future would be if I was telling her that I was gay. Maybe years of her also hearing from my doctors that I just needed a few procedures, that afterward I'd be able to get married to a man and have sex with him—I'd be normal—had taken a toll on her as well. Maybe she was just as caught up in the fantasy as the doctors were. Maybe she was in shock and the first thoughts that came to her mind were: *But do you still like guys? Is my daughter still my little girl? Is the girl who the doctors promised would be okay still on track to a happy, normal life?* I don't know. But jeez, that was some bad timing.

"Yeah, Mom, I mean, that's not the point!" I stammered, still in shock.

We went back and forth for a while, sometimes seemingly making progress and other times ending up right back at square one: my mom's guilt laced with self-preserving denial. I needed her comfort, but my mother seemed to be insisting that everything was fine, that what was done to deal with a "problem" had worked out for the best.

"Are you sure you can't feel anything down there?" she asked. "You said they cut you up down there? Your clitoris? I just can't believe that.

Your doctors were so wonderful and so nice. Families from all over the country were flying in to be seen by them. It just doesn't make any sense."

I rolled my eyes.

She continued: "They told your father and me that they were only going to cut a little bit of it away, just to make it a little bit smaller, and that's it. They said they were going to leave the nerves intact. Why would they lie?"

She said it as if she were asking God.

And then she lost it and broke down crying.

"There's gotta be something they can do?"

I was in no shape to continue the conversation. At least we'd broken through the first wave of total denial, but I obviously had not processed everything and didn't have the tools I needed to facilitate a conversation with my mother. I was hurt. I was scared. I was confused.

I reacted to everything I was feeling, all the rage bottled up inside, and stormed out of the kitchen. I ran up the stairs and threw myself facedown on Gram's bed.

My tears soaked into her pillowcase as Gram sat beside me, hushing me with her pursed lips, gently caressing my back with her smoothly gelled and lacquered nails. Back and forth, back and forth, back and forth.

As I lay there on her mattress, I felt even more alone. I knew the truth now, but I didn't know what to do with it. I felt like there was nobody in the world who would ever understand me—not even Mike. If my mom couldn't even understand me, how could I expect my boyfriend to? I dreaded the thought of telling him.

❦

The Flat Top Grill was located in a mall parking lot. It was a place where the cooks cook in front of you while you wait in line. Mikey and I both liked the orange chicken and rice. By that point, we had drifted so far apart from one another that our relationship hung on by only the scantest of threads. I was on the other side of town and busy with classes and my job. It had been easier than I expected to hide away from Mikey for the last half year or so.

But I needed to lift the weight off my shoulders and finally tell Mike what I had discovered. I was terrified of how he'd react to learning that his girlfriend had this weird intersex thing called androgen insensitivity syndrome. That I had to take pills every day to grow boobs. That I couldn't get pregnant. That I'd been lying to him for the past three and a half years every time I told him I couldn't have sex because I was on my period. On top of all that, I would have to tell him that I was born with XY chromosomes, undescended testes, and no uterus or ovaries. This was the thing I was most scared of revealing.

I had to tell my boyfriend I was a guy, or something like one.

I played and replayed possible scripts in my head.

Me: *Umm, Mike, I have something to tell you.*

Mike: *Okay?*

Me: *So, umm, I found out something about myself that I've been scared to tell you . . . I found out that I have this thing called androgen insensitivity syndrome, and it means that my body doesn't make estrogen. Instead, it makes androgens, like testosterone—well, it would have if they hadn't removed my undescended testes when I was a baby—and my body converts that testosterone, or would have, into estrogen. But since they removed my testes when I was a baby, I must take pills every day to give me hormones, and that's how I was able to grow these small boobs in junior high. Anyway, what I really wanted to tell you was that I don't get a period, I have no uterus or ovaries, and . . . well . . . ummm, I have XY chromosomes. 'K, bye.*

I envisioned Mike staring aghast at the mutant sitting across from him.

But that's not at all how it went down. Instead, while trying to fit the orange chicken in my stomach next to all the anxiety, I went over the game plan in my head. *Mikey, I love you. I have something to tell you. I need you to listen and not run away, okay? I need you to still love me after*

I tell you. Can you promise me you won't leave me? Can you promise that my truth won't change things? I'd practiced a million ways of saying it, of finally getting it off my chest.

Mikey had his fake ID and ordered a "brew," which was what he and his friends called beer. After three or four brews, he was buzzed. The familiar puffy red patches on his cheeks appeared, and I hardly recognized the boy I had fallen in love with four and a half years before.

"Can I get you two anything else?" our waiter asked us.

"Yes," Mike replied.

"No," I interjected.

"Another brew please," he said.

"Mike!" I said. "You have to drive us home!"

I was livid with him. Like my dad, he never knew when to stop drinking, and God forbid you demand they give you the car keys. It was like asking them to give you their kidney—it wasn't happening.

"Ready?" he asked.

"Yeah," I sighed.

Mikey and I had been fighting ever since, well, forever. Lately, though, something was changing inside of me; I no longer saw guys like Mikey as gods who were deserving of my devotion. We were on two different paths. While I was expanding, it seemed he was content with the status quo. The gap between us—both physically and emotionally— was getting harder to ignore. It also didn't help that pretty much all my new college friends didn't care for him either. The few times they'd met, it had not gone particularly well.

"You deserve someone better, sweetheart," Sabrina once told me. "Someone who doesn't become a raging, violent asshole every time he's drunk and high."

"He's not that bad," I replied. "He's just going through a lot right now with me being so far away. We spent practically every day with each other for three years. It's hard for him."

Sabrina, an Italian girl with big, piercing eyes and a penchant for theater, was not one to hold back. "What about you?" she said. "You don't deserve to be harassed with a million calls and texts and yelled at every time you're hanging out with your friends. You deserve someone who will worship the ground you walk on."

"He loves me," I replied. "He's just bad at showing it sometimes. He's got anger issues, but he says he's gonna work on it."

I said those things, but I knew in my heart it was over. Mike was Jennifer's boyfriend, but I was no longer Jennifer. I was becoming somebody else. And holding on to Mikey felt like I was holding on to a life that was no longer there. Sitting at the Flat Top Grill, I realized that I had to let that part of my life go.

I never did muster the courage to tell Mike that I was intersex. We continued to drift apart over the next few months, and then I ended it. I cried. I missed him. I second-guessed myself. And then I closed the door on that chapter of life forever.

CHAPTER 8

Back when I was first figuring things out, my seemingly endless Google searches led me to the Yahoo! New Rare Orchids Support Group for people like me, people born with AIS. When I found it, I felt confused by the name. *Was this a group about rare flowers?* After reading their bio, though, it became clear that orchids were a sort of mascot for the group's members, people who'd experienced orchiectomies, surgeries like mine that removed undescended testes. When I sat down to write my story and submit it so the group could verify if I was a legit orchid, it was the first time I had ever pieced together parts of my life for an audience. I was nervous to share such intimate details with strangers online, but I was promised that my words would be kept private. Privacy, I would soon learn, was integral to the New Rare Orchids.

Once I was let into the group, I was able to access the forums, where I saw questions and answers from people all over the country. I also gained access to the group's files, which included an ever-expanding collection of stories gathered from each new member. My eyes glazed over when I realized the document was eighty-seven tightly packed pages. Each story was unique, but each was an echo of my own. I read the document from beginning to end in one marathon sitting. I came away realizing that most of us had been harmed and lied to in exactly the same ways for close to half a century. It felt at once comforting and sad to be part of such a large group.

Soon after my fellow orchids let me in, my mother and I attended an annual in-person conference hosted by the group. We arrived at the front desk of the Palo Alto hotel where the conference was taking place, and I told the concierge that I was there for the orchids group. She looked at me with confusion. Just then, a tall, slender woman with a long face and wavy blonde ringlets arrived. I had seen her on the train earlier that day. She was alone and caught my eye. She placed her suitcase on the ground beside her and said, in an almost hushed voice, she was there for the "women's support group." The other concierge slid her a packet with an orchid sticker on it and welcomed her to the hotel. I took the cue and said I, too, was there for the *women's* support group. I got my packet and our room key, and we went upstairs.

The next morning, my mom and I ate breakfast, then set out to find the first session. There was a sign on the door that read WOMEN'S SUPPORT GROUP—SESSION A. Inside there were other women, all wearing orchid stickers that also read "Women's Support Group," with their names written in Sharpie above. I looked around and realized I was the youngest person in the room. Right before the first speaker started their presentation, someone in the audience raised their hand.

"Ummm, don't we need to close them?" she said as she nodded toward the shutters.

"Oh, yes, I almost forgot," the speaker responded.

She walked over to the white wooden shutters and closed each of them, leaving us lit by only her projector. I got the hint that we were going to talk about shameful things. When the presenter began speaking about AIS, she mentioned that often an early indicator that a *female* child has AIS is the appearance of a hernia, which subsequent surgical repair reveals to actually be an undescended testicle. I felt my mom tense up next to me as I remembered that my sister, Nicole, who was sixteen and still hadn't gotten her period, had a hernia operation when she was an infant.

"It's extremely rare for infants to get these types of hernias. They're almost always an indicator of AIS."

I then heard my mom sigh and say under her breath, "Oh no."

The presenter had also mentioned that AIS is hereditary and can present in multiple members of a family. We both realized that Nicole, who no one previously suspected was *different*, like me, might be. While part of me was excited thinking that I might be able to share this journey with Nicole, someone to weather the storm with, I could sense my mother didn't exactly feel the same way. While I understood that my mom's reaction came from a place of wanting to protect Nicole, it still stung. In that moment, I began to grasp why the shutters were closed.

After the presentations and sharing sessions, in which we passed around boxes of tissues and bawled our eyes out, we had social outings. During one of those nights on the town, at dinner in an Italian restaurant, the host complimented my looks. I was wearing mascara and a dress, and my hair was down and wavy. When he did that, the other orchids joined in and also began to praise all of my traits they thought were not only beautiful but also, more importantly, feminine.

"Your daughter has that perfect AIS skin!" one of the orchids told my mom.

It was understood among orchids that one of the benefits of not synthesizing androgens properly was clearer skin.

"And look at her big, beautiful eyes!" another chimed in.

"Gawd, what I'd do for those cheekbones!" someone else pointed out.

"Welcome home, beautiful girl," another person said quietly and smiled.

At one point, the host spoke up again and asked my mom if we were sisters. My mom loved when people asked us this, and with a big, playful grin on her face, she responded, "Yes!"

While it was very kind of everyone to say such nice things about my appearance, and to make my mom feel good in the process, something felt peculiar. I started to realize that even here, among those who were supposed to be my people, I felt odd. I started to get the feeling that the affirmations of the parts of me they viewed as feminine had a dual purpose: they were also affirmations of their own need to be seen as feminine. I started to realize that everyone there more or less wanted to fit the concept of what it meant to be a *normal* woman. One of the most common things expressed at that conference was sadness over one's vagina being too shallow or narrow for comfortable sex with men and also over the inability to give birth biologically. Everyone seemed sad that AIS prevented them from being able to conform to society's expectations of how women should behave and look. I wasn't so sure I wanted that anymore.

Learning I was intersex had opened me up to understanding myself, and sex and gender, in new and broader ways. When my mom and I left the conference, I felt both exhausted and filled with appreciation for being able to learn more and share my story for the first time in person with others like me—others who had similar journeys. I left with ambiguous feelings. I returned home feeling in some ways like a crew of one among a crew of many.

A couple of months later, I started my sophomore year of college, and I received an unexpected call from Lynnell. We had kept in touch over the last year, and our relationship had quickly grown into a genuine friendship. The embarrassed feelings I'd had about being seen in public with another intersex person had started to fade. Being around someone like Lynnell, who was so strong and proud of who they were, had started to rub off on me. I was no longer ashamed to be seen with Lynnell. In fact, the opposite was now true. I began to feel the first tinglings of pride about who I was.

After our initial pizza date, Lynnell and I began to hang out regularly. She had become like a big sister to me, an intersex big sister.

Following the conference, my mom scheduled a karyotype test for Nicole. It came back XX. She also got her period later that year, squashing any of my hopes that we would be AIS sisters. When I was with Lynnell, even though we weren't biologically related, I felt like she got me in a way no one else did, and like she had a shield that protected us from the world that had once tried so hard to hurt us.

"Hey, sis, guess what? I'm gonna be on *Oprah*!"

"What?"

"*Oprah*!"

"*The* Oprah?"

"Yes, *the* Oprah!"

"You're lying!"

"And guess what else?"

"What?"

"I can bring a guest."

"No."

"Yes! Do you want to come?"

"Stop it! *Me?*"

"*Yes!*"

"*On Oprah?!?*"

"*Yes!*"

"Oh my God! Praise Jesus!"

At that point, I was jumping up and down in my room and shouting into my phone like I'd just won a big ol' check from Publishers Clearing House. I grabbed last semester's syllabus off my desk and scribbled down the details.

Tues., Sept. 18, 10 a.m. OPRAH!!!

Growing up, the phrase I remember hearing the most in my house was: *Shhhh, Oprah's on!* This was followed by: *Did you hear about Oprah and Stedman?* Or: *Do you think she's dating Gayle?* Or: *Did you see how much weight Oprah gained?* Which was, of course, always followed by: *Oh my God, did you see how much weight Oprah lost?* You see, Oprah was almost sacred in our home. There was not a single person in my entire family who didn't love Oprah. In fact, Oprah was like another member of our family. We saw her more often than most of our distant relatives, who were scattered around the country. Besides the Chicago Bulls, nothing made us prouder of our city than Oprah. And even though she recorded her show in the city, just a few miles from where we lived, I never knew anybody who'd been to a taping.

The night before Lynnell was scheduled to be on *Oprah*, I couldn't sleep at all. I stared at the ceiling, my body jittery with excitement, like a little kid waiting for Santa on Christmas Eve.

It was another milestone: I was the first person in my family to go to college, and now, almost more importantly, I was about to become the first person to be in Oprah's audience.

I woke up flushed. Nerves and excitement buzzed through my body. My mind was racing with questions for the Queen of Chicago: *What should I wear? Will I be seated toward the front, where my family can see me? Will I ask a question? What should I ask? Will I get to meet Oprah?*

I jumped out of bed, hopped into the shower, and let the warm water cascade over my body, hoping that the steam and heat would heal my anxious heart and tired bones. I wrung my hair with a towel before whipping it up into a messy bun, then picked out my best pair of Abercrombie jeans and my favorite sky-blue sweater. I forced myself to go to class, but how did they expect me to focus on English lit when today belonged to Oprah? I decided I would sit in their classroom, fine, but my mind and my spirit would be elsewhere, blocks away, in a little place called Harpo Studios.

At 9:15 a.m., while daydreaming about riding ponies with Oprah, I got a text from Lynnell: Running early. Be outside at 9:45! Don't be late!!

I closed my notebook and quietly zipped up my backpack, sneaking out of my class without any type of explanation. When I stepped out into the hallway, it was so quiet that you could hear a pin drop. No one was around. I pushed the heavy glass door open to exit the building, and the students I'd imagined would be packed into the quad, looking on in awe and gawking at me as I casually stepped into a sleek limousine, courtesy of Harpo Studios, after my class ended, were nowhere to be found. Besides two squirrels who were chasing each other, not a single soul witnessed my royal pickup.

But I am here to say that it happened. A black limo pulled up, the driver opened the back door for me, and I crouched to get in.

"Welcome to my limo, baby," Lynnell said gleefully as I hugged her. There were twinkly lights in the felt ceiling, and an unopened bottle of champagne was sweating on ice in between us.

"I can't believe this!" I squealed. "Thank you for inviting me!"

"Oprah, here we come!" Lynnell said with a huge smile, dimples in full view. "Here we come!"

❦

Harpo Studios—where Oprah's show was taped—was in the West Loop. And though the studio was only a few miles from the places where I had grown up on the far Northwest Side and Elmwood Park, it existed in an entirely different galaxy of swanky restaurants and warehouses converted into fancy condominiums. Two completely different worlds. Harpo Studios felt like Emerald City—some magical place I'd heard existed, on TV, and was just out there in the distance. I'm not sure I ever really believed it was real until I saw it that day.

It took only fifteen minutes before our limo began to slow.

I could see the Harpo Studios sign on a nearby corner with a big, tilted O on top. Beyond the sign was a behemoth building with a massive corner crafted out of curved, undulating glass blocks. Stacked on top of that were three giant concentric metal hoops that gave way to a spire reaching into the airwaves.

Before I knew what was happening, Lynnell and I were being whisked into the building. At some point in all the chaos, I got separated from Lynnell—she was ushered into a green room for Oprah's guests, and I was swept up in a stampede of tourists and suburban homemakers who were corralled together like cattle in the stockyards. And, hey, if we could achieve our shared dream of becoming *Oprah* audience members, none of us seemed to mind.

It looked to me like I was the only one who was there alone. Without anyone to talk to, I stood wondering whether Lynnell had met Oprah yet while producers rushed by assigning people seat numbers. Then they finally let us into the studio.

I felt a strange mix of excitement and letdown as I saw the stage for the first time. I couldn't believe how small the studio was! It looked so much bigger on Gram's TV. Stepping into the sacred space took me back to the time when I first realized that my cartoons didn't actually live inside the TV. There were rows of regular folding chairs. The studio was small and beige. I was like Dorothy peeking behind the curtain and discovering that the Great and Powerful Oz was just a tiny, little bald man. Sitting in that magicless space and waiting for the show to begin sucked a minuscule amount of excitement out of the experience.

But on the bright side, I knew that pretty soon I wouldn't be too far from Oprah.

◆◆◆◆◆

The tourists and gaggle of moms shuffled in. They were smiling, laughing. Snapping photos of each other with the empty stage behind them. They were over the moon to be scratching something off their bucket lists. They'd come to be entertained.

And that's when it hit me: I was there for a different reason. I was there because I was intersex, and because Lynelle wanted me to experience the discussion between intersex people—a moment in which our reality was going to be acknowledged and broadcast to millions of at-home viewers.

I suddenly felt even more alone. I'd walked in thinking I'd been given access to something that I'd never dreamed could happen to me—and that was still true—but I was only there because I was so different, because I was a part of a community that no one understood. By that time, I was used to feeling like the odd one out. It's how I usually felt around other people. But I hadn't expected the feeling to creep up on this unbelievable day.

I was ushered to a seat way off in a back corner, far from the cameras, so there would be no way Gram, my mom, or anyone in my family, for that matter, would see me on TV.

Welp, I thought, *there go my five seconds of fame.*

Minutes later, people with black headsets swept across the stage, and a producer named Joyce welcomed us to the show. "Hello, everybody! It's so nice to meet you! I'm Joyce, and I'm going to walk you through everything you need to know. But first, make some noise if this is your first time at *The Oprah Showww!*"

The audience erupted into thunderous applause. Hooting and hollering like their heads were going to fall off. Joyce continued to make small talk with us before directing our attention to the applause signs above us.

"Let's practice," she said.

We began clapping our hands on cue. It all felt so forced, so manufactured. A little bit more of the magic faded away.

But then, just when I started to feel a bit cynical about the experience, Joyce asked us the question we'd all been waiting for: "Who is ready to meet Oprah?"

The woman beside me let out a squeal. The room exploded with applause. The curtain slowly opened. And there she was. The queen herself.

It was Oprah.

I may be misremembering this next detail, but I'm pretty sure she was shrouded in a holy glowing aura as she walked onto the stage.

Angels were singing. There was a cherub playing a harp. It was something of a religious experience.

Oprah waved hello while dazzling us with her trademark warm smile. And we were all chanting together as one: "Oprah! Oprah! Oprah!" The air had become electrified. The magic was real. My heart was pounding, and I couldn't believe I was in a room with the queen of daytime television. In that moment, everyone and everything around me melted away. All I could see was Oprah.

Oprah spoke to us like we were old friends. She had the comforting approachability of a therapist or a favorite teacher. I felt like I could walk up to her and cry on her shoulder. She even cracked some jokes to loosen up the crowd, and then, out of nowhere, her mood jolted into a fit of brief rage. She snapped her fingers, and suddenly it was like we weren't there anymore. She focused on someone in her glam squad: "Lashes!" she cried, and a makeup artist rushed to fix her eyelashes.

Oh, wow, I thought. *She really is the* queen *of daytime television.* Impressive.

The studio lights went dim as the stage lights grew bright. A woman with a clipboard began counting down from ten. And then it began, the episode of *Oprah* that would change the trajectory of my life.

The first two guests were a young, blonde white woman named Katie and her mom, Arlene. Katie looked like the poster child for white, well-to-do America. From the audience, I studied Katie's svelte, oval-shaped face. She had brown eyes and pouty pink lips. Everything about her dainty facial features screamed feminine—and a bit tense. I couldn't help but try to imagine what she looked like without her straight, shoulder-length blonde hair. I tried to squint and imagine her with a shaved head, wondering if she looked like a boy underneath her hair and makeup.

Oprah introduced her by showing the audience a prerecorded video that featured Katie speaking about the trials and tribulations of growing up intersex. The video package included photographs of Katie as a beaming young girl twirling a baton in her band uniform.

At one point in the video, she said, "The hardest thing was knowing that all of these doctors who'd come into my exam room when I was a kid had known a lot more about my body than I did. That was difficult, to feel like there was this secret about my body that I wasn't in on, and that my private parts were public."

I shifted nervously in my seat when I heard those words. Even my bones were paying attention. She was telling my story. When the video stopped rolling and the lights came up, Katie and her mom reappeared onstage next to Oprah.

Oprah began sharing how difficult it was for her producers to book guests for this show about being intersex because most people don't want to talk about it. They want to keep their secrets. They don't want the scrutiny.

I shifted again. I felt a sharp pang rip across my stomach. A visceral reminder that I still hadn't told anyone in my life except my mom. It was all hitting a little too close to home.

Katie explained that she decided to go public with her story in the hopes of making it easier for women like herself to be able to talk about this someday. She said she wanted to lift the shroud of secrecy that covers so many lives. I'm a bit ashamed to admit this today, but when Katie reaffirmed that she, and others like her, were *women*, I felt a sense of relief, as if my racing mind let out a deep exhale.

"So, genetically, you are male?" Oprah asked.

Katie kept her composure and responded.

"In a sense I am because I have an X chromosome and a Y chromosome. And what happened was, the Y chromosome told my body to develop testes, but when my testes were functioning like they're supposed to, producing lots and lots of male hormones, like testosterone, my body just didn't respond to them because I'm insensitive to androgens. That's where the name androgen insensitivity syndrome comes from. So, in a sense, I'm not a male at all, because I'm producing all these hormones . . ."

"But you do have testes . . ."

"I *did* have testes."

I took a deep, Lamaze-like breath and tried to keep cool as my heart thumped in my chest cavity. Like Katie, I *did* have testes too. But unlike her, I was not yet ready to tell anyone—let alone Oprah! The word *testes* was enough to trigger me into a spiral of shame about who or what I was. I could barely bring myself to think about it, let alone say it out loud. Thinking of myself as a girl who was born with testes made me queasy. And here the conversations I'd been avoiding were playing out right before me—and on national TV.

"You did . . ."

"Right," Katie said. "They were removed."

I could feel heat and anger blazing through my body. My face was hot, and my breath was restricted, like I was forgetting how to extract oxygen from the air.

Oprah shifted too. "How is your body not like a normal female body? Or is it?"

"The only thing that's different is that inside, instead of ovaries, I had these testes, and I never developed a uterus or fallopian tubes or cervix."

"Okay, but when you say inside, can we use the vajayjay word?" Oprah asked.

Oprah said vajayjay!

I memorialized that moment properly in my mind and then immediately went back to having a quiet nervous breakdown as I watched my life be examined and picked apart in front of me.

"I mean inside my body," Katie said. "In most women, what happens is the vagina leads to a canal in the uterus so babies and menstrual blood can come out."

Oprah then asked her, point blank, whether she had a vagina or not. Katie said yes. *I have a vajayjay.*

Oprah fist-bumped Katie, and the crowd erupted with laughter. Everyone except me. My body shifted again in the folding chair, readjusting for the third time, writhing because my intersex-sympathy neurons were firing.

Oprah meant well.

I know she was trying to find a common ground. She was going for a girl-power moment. All of us as one, united by our common denominator, the Great and Powerful Vajayjay. But her intentions and consequences didn't quite align.

Oprah had inadvertently reduced the entirety of Katie and her womanhood to a single body part. And not just any body part but the crème de la crème: the vagina.

And while Oprah didn't then use a scalpel to continue shaping Katie into her narrow definition of what a normal woman is, Oprah did reaffirm to her millions of viewers that gender determination lives between the flesh of one's thighs.

Oprah continued.

"How do you tell people that you're genetically male, or do you?"

"I shared a little bit in high school," Katie said. "But it was difficult because a lot of people just didn't understand it. So I got teased about it. And that was really difficult."

"How can you get teased if nobody understands what it is?"

"When you tell someone you don't have a uterus, the logical question is: Where did it go? And I didn't know the answer to that. So they would say I was mutated. Or a mutant."

"Did you ever feel mutated? Did you feel like a mutant?"

I fought back the tears that were welling in my eyes.

"Of course," she said. "So much of adolescence for a girl is moving through these rites of passage: getting your period, buying your first bra, having your parent be awkward about it, going on your first date. All this stuff I wasn't really doing at the same time my friends were. I felt really isolated. I had never met anyone else like me. It's very lonely."

And with that, I felt a tear drip from my eyelash and slide down my cheek into the corner of my mouth.

"And when did you start to then not feel so isolated or lonely about it?"

"The best thing that ever happened to me, with respect to this, was when I was eighteen. My parents took me to my first androgen insensitivity syndrome support group meeting, and I met some really amazing, talented, beautiful, smart women who were just like me."

It was a commercial break.

Good, I thought. I needed one.

Oprah introduced her next guest. "Thirty-nine-year-old Hida says she feels blessed to be born intersex."

Hida was androgynous in a way that made me pay attention. They had tan skin, a short fauxhawk, and an athletic build. I instantly developed a crush on them. They sat onstage with an air of confidence as they shared that they were born with an enlarged clitoris, though hadn't been operated on, unlike me. As they shared details about their *blessed* intersex life, I was given a new perspective on what intersex people's lives could be like, if we were all given bodily autonomy.

In fact, there was a segment in which Oprah was speaking to a doctor who advocated for intersex rights. During their talk, the doctor was arguing for less medical intervention and said the best course of action "[s]ometimes . . . mean[t] accepting the child the way that they are." Hida, who wasn't part of that planned segment, interrupted to confidently say, "*Always* that means accepting the child the way that they are." Hida went on to explain that there are no studies showing that being intersex is a health risk or a detriment. And then they followed it up with the kicker: "I feel blessed. I would not be a 'regular woman' if you paid me." It was thrilling to hear them embracing their identity so absolutely. After Hida wrapped up their interview, something dawned on me. Before this moment, I was worried that if I ever went public with my story, people would shun me. But after hearing Hida share their story, two things happened: my fondness for them grew, and I realized that maybe I could share my story as well one day.

Then Oprah's voice-over began to speak. "When she was just two days old, doctors sewed her up and made her into a boy. Her story is next." Up next was Lynnell.

Lynnell was a lot of things to me. She inspired me to find some light at the end of this tunnel. I admired her bravery and ability to go around sharing her story with hundreds of people, to make the world a better place for future kids born like us, born intersex, but that quality I admired also scared the hell out of me.

In my state of fear, I was still doing the work of the doctors who wished to erase from us everything that made us intersex. Prejudices about people like Lynnell, people who were different, were wedged deep in the folds of my cerebellum, where they had been long before I discovered who or what I was. In shunning others, I was simultaneously crucifying myself—one nail at a time.

Everything about how I viewed the world around me had crumbled beneath my feet during those last few months. Even though everything seemed to be shifting, and nothing felt stable, there was one thing I felt certain about: that I didn't want anyone to ever find out about my truth. The thought alone was suffocating.

Lynnell took her seat. She looked different. I had never seen even a smidge of makeup on her face before, but today it was caked in a heavy layer of powder and rosy blush. After the show, she would tell me that she felt like the producers had put her in femme drag and that before she walked onstage, she had wiped as much of the thick makeup off as she could.

Lynnell had been invited on this show to speak her truth, but still the producers were trying to hide her under clothes and makeup she'd never wear. Just as the doctors had made surgical changes that molded Lynnell to fit their own limited scope of gender, the producers were now doing a less severe version of the same thing: caking makeup onto

Lynnell's face so she'd appear more feminine—when their true self presented as masculine.

Lynnell was butch, a dom, the reigning International Mr. Leather. Yet there she was, in femme garb—lipstick and a flowy silk button-up. The producers, like the doctors, wanted to make Lynnell's decision for her. It was about their own comfort, not Lynnell's. It reflected their narrow and binary view of what a person could be and should look like, feelings be damned. Seeing her like that, so different from her day-to-day way of expressing herself, made me wonder if she was uncomfortable.

The assumption society has that one's sex and gender are binary and plainly obvious was on full display. We are raised to believe that you should just be able to glance at someone for a split second and know what lies between not only their legs but also their ears. On top of this, there is also supposed to be an inherent synchronicity between the two.

Masculine facial features and dress? He obviously has a penis and testicles and identifies as a man. Feminine facial features and dress? She obviously has a vagina, a uterus, and ovaries, and she also identifies as a woman. Period. It's obvious. Nuance be damned.

As I sat there waiting for the commercial break to end and Lynnell's segment to begin, I couldn't believe these medieval surgical procedures had happened to me. Even worse, I couldn't believe they were still happening to others.

I listened to Lynnell's pretaped video: "My name is Lynnell Stephani Long," she said. "My birth certificate originally says Stephen Lynnell Long. I was born with genitalia that is not necessarily male or female. My chromosomes were XY, which is supposed to be of a male."

It was a three-minute summary of Lynnell's life. She was born with hypospadias—a condition in which one's urethra doesn't open from the tip of one's phallus—and with a vaginal opening. But since there was no vaginal canal, the doctors sewed her vagina together and pronounced her a baby boy. She began growing breasts during puberty. She said it felt torturous. When she was fourteen years old and in high school, she was taking showers with the boys. The doctors told her she was a boy. Her mother told her she was a boy. But her body said no. Her body knew something didn't make sense.

Then the studio lights faded on again. The video ended, and Oprah spoke.

"Today we're talking to people who were born intersex," she said. "It's the term that is preferred by the community. A lot of us are more familiar with the term *hermaphrodite*. But hermaphrodite is not what people wish to be called. So the word is *intersex*. It means you have parts of both male and female sexual organs. It's biological.

"Lynnell, how long did you live as Steve?"

"Thirty years," Lynnell replied.

"Thirty years?!"

"A long time."

"A long time," said Oprah. "Did you feel tortured or repressed?"

"I thought I was schizophrenic," Lynnell said. "I felt like there was this person deep down dying to come out, and on the outside was this facade that was just waiting to go away."

"It's confusing to people who haven't experienced it," Oprah said. "Many people are reading about it for the first time in the book I chose for the summer: *Middlesex* by Jeffrey Eugenides. Let me ask you: Did you feel gay?"

"Gay?" Lynnell asked. She seemed kind of shocked.

"Gay," Oprah replied flatly.

"Gay? Like homosexual?" Lynnell asked again.

Oprah nodded.

"I am gay," Lynnell said. "*Gay* is a good word for me."

Oprah dug in.

"Okay, but as a boy. Living as Steve. You were also gay?"

Lynnell sighed, and the crowd laughed. It was about to get even more complicated.

"Yes," Lynnell said. "When I was Steve, I felt like a homosexual. I felt like a gay guy. Very effeminate. No masculinity to me at all. I felt like a gay man, yes."

"But your mother and the doctors insisted you were a man?"

"Yes."

"Did you feel like you were a woman inside a man's body? Or did you just feel like you were gay?"

"I felt like a woman inside a man's body. I wouldn't use *gay* to describe me when I was young. I would use *feminine*. I got called the F-word a lot. I got called a lot of names because I didn't act like the other boys. Boys are supposed to be tough, but that wasn't me at all. I would rather play with dolls and jump rope."

"What was the turning point?"

"For ten years I was addicted to drugs and alcohol," Lynnell said. "That was no life at all. I wasn't living at all. I was very asexual and just wanted to die. So then when I got off drugs and alcohol, I decided to start living."

"What gave you the courage?" Oprah asked.

"I got sober."

"Were the drugs and alcohol because you were trying to make yourself live as Steve?"

"Yes. I thought if I got married, I could really be a guy. I couldn't have kids, but she had a kid, and I could be a stepfather—"

Oprah cut in. "And finally fulfill this role that you had been told your whole life?"

"Yes. Exactly. And it didn't work."

After the show ended and the lights went up, I sat in my chair while the audience filed out. The thought of other babies going through what we went through, even after these brave people bared their souls to the world with such vulnerability, was making my blood boil.

My heart was certain that I had to do something to make this nightmare stop. But my mind was not so sure. My mind screamed, trying to convince my heart: *No one will love you if they find out! Everyone will point and laugh at you. They'll call you a freak. They'll spit on you and kick dust in your face. You'll regret coming out every second for the rest of your life.*

But after seeing Katie and Lynnell on Oprah, I felt inspired to go public with my story, and hopefully help other intersex kids in the process. I wanted to be brave like Katie and Lynnell.

CHAPTER 9

Two weeks after I turned twenty, I kissed a girl.

Ashley Vento was butch and blue eyed, with a lip ring and a thick Boston accent. Before she kissed me, I'd just assumed I was straight. But then Ashley Vento came into my life and swept me off my feet.

Ashley had the cutest patch of freckles that spanned from one cheek to the other, and she always wore an expertly rolled bandanna tied up as a headband in her short hair.

She wore a variation of the same thing every day: Nike Dunks, jeans, a T-shirt, a studded belt, a black North Face fleece—if it was cool—and that bandanna. The bandanna held back most of her hair, but it always seemed to let a swoop of angled golden bangs fall over her eyes. She rolled her own cigarettes and smoked like a chimney. And she wore a hemp necklace adorned with a glass bead.

She was perfect.

Her apartment was right across the street from Wrigley Field and right next to the Red Line tracks. It was on the top floor, and if you stuck your hand out of her bedroom window, you could almost touch the train. It was our secret nest in the middle of the city. Every time the train sped by, her bedroom floor would rumble, and the TV would become inaudible. When we were up there, the rest of the world faded away.

Before she kissed me, I told myself that we were just friends. We met in sociology class during my sophomore year. She moved from her usual seat to the seat next to mine.

People moved around a lot, I thought to myself. *No biggie.*

But then we started talking and got to know each other. She had an amazing smile that made her eyes light up and a loud and unapologetic cackle. Eventually we started hanging out after class and spending lots of time together.

I made a new friend, I thought.

One afternoon, before I was supposed to grab some food and study for sociology with Ashley in the student center, I took a lot of time to get ready. I showered, did my hair and makeup, stressed over what to wear before finally settling on what I hoped was a cute outfit, and then sprayed myself with perfume. My reflection in the mirror seemed to look back at me with a devilish grin.

Eventually, one thing led to another, and one night we were spooning on my bottom bunk. Then one morning we were making out in her bed. Immediately after she kissed me for the first time, I turned away and buried my face in her pillow. My cheeks flushed, and I panicked.

Oh my God, I just kissed a girl, I thought. *What the fuck is happening?*

"Are you okay?" she gently asked.

I took a second. Then I turned my head to face her and nodded with a smile. From that moment on, I was hooked. For the next six months, we never left each other's sides. Ashley made me feel desired in a way I had never experienced before. I loved how her eyes devoured my entire being every time she looked at me. I felt completely alive in that way that you do when you are on a good roller coaster. Feeling that alive was addictive. I couldn't get enough.

One afternoon, Ashley opened up and told me about her past.

"I used to be addicted to heroin, but I stopped right around the time I met you," she told me. I hate to say it, but learning that made me feel a weird sense of pride.

I looked down at her arms and saw for the first time that they were covered in scars; the marks looked like flesh-colored snakes sleeping on each other for warmth. She noticed me looking and then said, "Oh yeah, and I used to cut, but I've stopped that too."

The things she shared with me, which to some might have seemed like red flags, just made me fall in love with her even harder. Her vulnerability made me feel closer to her. Her past, for some messed-up, probably codependent reason, made me feel safe.

Two weeks after our first kiss, we went for a walk together, in love, unable to stop looking into each other's eyes. We eventually drifted from DePaul's campus and started walking down Fullerton Avenue toward the lake. We passed the Dominick's grocery store and kept meandering toward the six-corner intersection where Fullerton, Lincoln, and Halsted all crisscrossed. As we passed the driveway leading up to the front doors of Lurie Children's Hospital, I squeezed her hand tighter. We finally made it to our destination just as the moon was beginning to rise. Up ahead, the waves crashed onto the sandy shores of Lake Michigan. As the moon inched higher, we walked closer to the shore, like two baby sea turtle hatchlings about to enter the silky, dark unknown. We stood still, staring into the horizon that separated water from sky. It was almost impossible to perceive where one ended and the other began.

"Tell me your story," Ashley said as we held hands in the twilight. "I want to know your life story, boo."

She gave my hand a gentle squeeze.

The sound of my heart palpitations was masked only by the whoosh of the waves. She had been asking me to tell her my life story for a while now, and each time she asked, I became sick with fear. That familiar lump, a glue trap lodged in my throat, rarely allowed the escape of any words.

If I shared my secret with Ashley, there would be no going back.

My bones were yearning to take the jump, to finally confide in someone, but my mind was screaming: *Caution, caution, red alert!*

The stars did their little dance in the sky as Ashley and I walked away from the edge of the water and sat down on a bench behind the bike path. My heart thumped, my head pounded, and my eyes began to well up. Ashley's nicotine-yellowed fingers caressed my hair under the cool light of a waning gibbous moon.

"Shhh . . . it's okay, boo. I'm not going nowhere. Nevah. You can tell me. Whatevah it is, I love you."

She wiped away a tear that had begun rolling down my cheek.

"Fuck," I cried out. And then, like water from a collapsed dam, it all came pouring out.

"If I tell you something, you promise you won't run away?" I sniffled.

"I promise," she said. She looked like she meant it.

"When I was born, they thought I was a girl. But when I was six months old, they found out I had XY chromosomes."

I couldn't believe this was happening. I was sure that I was going to screw up our relationship. At the same time, cathartic endorphins drenched my brain, and I decided to keep sharing.

"When I was a baby, they took out my undescended testes," I said. "They castrated me."

I am making a huge mistake, I thought. *I should stop.* I tried to read Ashley's face to see if she was horrified. But to my surprise, she wasn't. Her eyes were understanding and inviting. I took solace in how I read her eyes. I continued.

"When I was four . . . they . . . they . . . they cut off . . . my clitoris," I said between choky gasps for oxygen.

"I'm so sorry that happened to you," Ashley said as she kissed my forehead.

I turned and sobbed into the soft fleece of her North Face. And then I told her the rest.

"They lied! They lied to me about everything," I howled at the moon. "Everyone lied."

I shuddered in her lap, ready for her to stand up any second and say, "Yeah, no, I'm sorry, but I gotta go. This is too much."

I was ready for a look of disgust to flash across her face when she registered what she had been tricked into falling in love with. I closed my eyes, tightened every muscle in my body, and braced myself for whatever was coming next.

But she didn't run away. She didn't scream in horror. Instead, she squeezed me tighter, kissed me on the forehead, and said, "If you had three testes and one boob, I'd still love you, boo."

And for the first time in what felt like forever, my heart took a deep breath and exhaled it all out into the Milky Way.

CHAPTER 10

About a month after I met Ashley, I found out what she was majoring in. "You major in what?" I asked.

"Women's and gendah studies," she nonchalantly replied, like it was the most ordinary major in the world. I loved when she had to say words that ended in *-er*. Her Boston accent was the cutest.

"What the hell is that?" I asked her. "What do you study?"

"Feminism and queer theory and stuff like that," she said, except she said *queer* with her accent, so it sounded more like *qwee-yah*!

When I began DePaul, I declared digital cinema as my major. About a year into the filmmaking program, I got curious about what else was out there. I had been feeling academically directionless for a while, bouncing around from possible major to possible major. If the major ended in *-ogy*, chances were good that I had at least taken an intro class in it.

With all of my dibble-dabbling in any major that sounded remotely interesting during my first two years of college, I had never even heard of women's and gender studies. Probably because it didn't end in *-ogy*.

"It's amazing," she said, beaming with pride. "I love my professahs. Oh my God, you have to meet them."

"Feminism?" I asked.

I rolled the word around in my head and thought back to my favorite high school teacher, Ms. Bocio. Ms. Bocio was the epitome of cool.

She didn't care about the strict conventions of our conservative Catholic high school. How did I know this? Well, for starters, unlike every other teacher, she always came to work looking like she had just rolled out of bed—just like many of us students. Secondly, she was always there to help us avoid detention by writing us fake tardy passes. And lastly, she openly talked with us about her love of smoking pot, she didn't shave her armpits, and she had a tattoo of the female symbol that she told us represented feminism.

But after her, I had never heard much else about feminists or feminism until I met Ashley.

One afternoon, a few weeks after Ashley and I professed our love to one another, she invited me to a student club meeting with her.

"Boo, come with me to FIA!" Ashley insisted while we were making out in the library stacks. "I want my friends to see how pretty my boo is."

I would discover that FIA! was the acronym for a student group on campus called Feminists in Action! The group met on the mezzanine level of the student center.

Everyone in FIA! was either majoring or minoring in women's and gender studies.

When we got there, everyone was sitting in a circle, some on pulled-up comfy chairs and others on the floor. Ashley and I showed up late because we'd been making out in the elevator, and then in the hallway, and then outside the door of the meeting room. We stumbled in all drunk on the sweet taste of being young and in love. Everyone turned to us when we arrived.

"Ventooo!" the group cheered.

"Hi, everyone," Ashley said through a huge grin. "Sorry I've been MIA. But I have a good reason."

Then she turned toward me and said, "Everyone, this is my girl-friend, Jen."

"Aww!"

My hands went clammy, and my stomach began to churn. I didn't always like meeting new people, and my belly decided—as it often did—to protest by depositing painful pockets of gas in the chambers of my intestines. I was picking up on the fact that my life was about to radically shift. I was yearning to be a part of this promised feminist world, where people studied feminism and embraced different ideals of sex and gender, ones that existed outside of the binary. Something about it felt necessary, almost like a calling. Ultimately, I desired what Ashley had: passion and purpose.

"Hi," I meekly replied. My grip on Ashley's hand became tighter.

"Isn't she pretty?" Ashley said. There were stars in her eyes. I felt like the center of her universe, and it was nerve-racking and exhilarating.

"Sit downnn, Vento," someone said, chuckling.

We took our seats on the floor, and as we did, someone with luscious black curls and big, round brown eyes offered me a pillow to sit on.

They look familiar, I thought to myself as I took the group in.

"Thank you," I said, wondering where I had seen these people before.

A tiny person with a pronounced nose and cute, shoulder-length blond curls began the meeting. They introduced themself as H.

"Today's check-in question is, if you were a sea creature, which sea creature would you be?" H said with the cadence of a cool, unbothered manatee. I liked the way they talked.

"Oh, and don't forget to say your names and pronouns."

Shoot, I thought. I began to panic. I suddenly hated this. The moments leading up to my turn, especially among new people, were always so fraught for me. Upon hearing the very words *check-in,* my stomach launched a counterattack against my attempts to calm it. I clenched my sphincter with all the strength I had and prayed.

Please, please, please don't let me fart in front of my new people, I thought to myself.

The person with black curls and a kind face checked in next.

"Umm, let's see, if I were a sea creature," they said, stretching out the word *creature* while thinking of their answer in the most adorable way, "I'd probably be either a sea lion or a walrus. They look like they know how to chill."

Everyone chuckled and nodded in agreement.

"Oh, and my name is Flowers, and I use they/them pronouns."

They, who, what?! I thought. I was confused. I had never heard anyone use these pronouns before. In fact, I had never really thought about pronouns before. I had just always assumed you were either she or he; you didn't get a choice in the matter, and that was that. A bead of sweat formed in the hollow between my breasts. And now I was in full-out panic mode because not only couldn't I think of a sea creature that somehow completely conveyed the entirety of my personality to these strangers, but now I also had to pretend like I hadn't just heard someone say their pronouns were *they* and *them*.

I looked at Ashley, and she was completely laid back, like a sea lion on the beach. I needed an escape plan.

If I go to the bathroom right before it's my turn, maybe they'll skip me, I thought. Escape this pressure and release another pressure in one calculated move! The plan seemed promising.

But right before I shifted my weight in order to stand up, I was busted. It was too late to escape.

Flowers pointed at me and said, "Your turn!"

I could feel everyone's eyes turn toward me.

Shoot! I couldn't believe my luck.

"Oh, it's my turn?" I said, trying to stall. "Hmm, if I were a sea creature, what would I be? Hmm . . ."

I started to feel flushed. A couple of days after my most recent bladder surgery, when I was eleven, the nurses told me one morning that I had to get up that day and walk. When I did as they wished, I almost immediately blacked out and woke up back in my gurney with a cold washcloth on my forehead and a nurse telling me to drink an orange juice—the kind with the crinkly tinfoil top. Before I blacked out, I felt my blood pressure drop and the world start to fade away. I felt similar in this moment. My stomach launched another attack on my small intestine as I tried to think of a sea creature.

"A sea turtle!" I blurted out. "I love sea turtles."

Relieved, I tried to get comfortable by shifting my sitting position while taking great care not to release any biological weapons upon the group.

Who should I pick to go next? I wondered to myself as I scanned the circle before being interrupted by H.

"And what's your pronoun?" they asked.

"Oh, right, my pronoun," I replied. "I, umm, my pronouns are . . ." I was buying time while the words *46 XY male pseudo-hermaphrodite* flashed across my mind's eye.

46 XY male pseudo-hermaphrodite.

Undescended gonads.

Enlarged clitoris.

"Umm, I use she?"

My tone blurred the line between an answer and a question. No one had ever asked me what my pronouns were before. I'd never asked myself. I suddenly felt like I needed to do a more thorough check-in with myself.

DePaul required all sophomores to take an interdisciplinary class. In filling out my schedule, I randomly ended up in a class taught by a women's and gender studies (WGS) faculty member, Dr. Laila Farah. The class was called Immigrants or "Alien Others"? From the moment Laila walked into our classroom, I took notice. She had big hazel eyes accentuated with blue eyeliner, a rectangular-oval face, and long, golden waves of hair. She wore silk scarves that seemed to hover all around her, suspended in air. I was hooked. Then she spoke.

"I"—she took a beat—"am Dr. Laila Farah"—another dramatic beat—"and this is ISP 200," she concluded. "Welcome."

Wow. Who is this lady? Laila had a background in theater. She was a veteran of one-person shows and knew how to command a room. She floated in like a shining star.

Besides being completely captivated by Laila's iconic presence, I was enthralled by our reading assignments and class discussions. It was post 9/11, and the readings introduced me to deconstructing racist tropes. They challenged the ways in which I was conditioned to see *others*. They encouraged me to question an us-versus-them mentality. There was hardly a binary paradigm left unexplored. There were heated debates and long, lively discussions.

⁂

For the first time in my life, my way of thinking about the world and many of its issues wasn't grounds for an argument with someone in my family. Instead, it was helping me get good grades on assignments.

Each class made me feel alive!

But I also started to feel like I had an impossible future.

I feared my family would throw a fit when they found out I was putting my father and myself into debt to graduate as a professional feminist. I could already envision the heart attack my grandmother would have upon realizing that the granddaughter whom she had poured her hopes and dreams into, believing that I'd be the first in the family to go to college and become a doctor or a lawyer, had instead obtained a degree in radical lesbian Marxism, with few high-paying job prospects.

I'd never felt so engaged and so sure that my work could be urgent and personal. The next day, I declared my major. Women's and gender studies.

I was on my way to finding my purpose.

After I declared my major, I gradually started exploring ways in which I could personally challenge the gender binary. In time, I stopped shaving my leg hair and the hair under my armpits. I also began to cut my hair shorter and shorter. When I first learned I was intersex, I had so many urgent issues to confront that my hair was the last thing on my mind. When I met Ashley, I had shoulder-length hair. But after a year or so, I began making slow, incremental changes, until one night, on a whim, I asked Ashley to shave my head in my apartment's tiny bathroom. My obsession with Natalie Portman and her shaved head in *V for Vendetta* had finally come full circle. It was done.

Staring at myself with my freshly buzzed head, I was in a state of shock fueled by an increasingly recurring thought: *My family's going to kill me.* But as I stared longer, tracing the new contours of my head, I flashed back to the moment, just a year and a half before, when I first read the words *46 XY male pseudo-hermaphrodite* in my medical records and pulled my hair back with my palm to see if, underneath it all, I was actually a boy. I couldn't believe how much had changed since that moment. Back then, I had made a pact with myself that I would never tell anyone what I'd just read. I was terrified of anyone knowing I wasn't really a girl. That I wasn't *normal*.

And here I was looking in the mirror again, and instead of drowning in a puddle of shame, I was standing tall and barefoot in fluffy piles of my discarded tendrils, enjoying the uniquely satisfying sensation of rubbing my hand over the Velcro of what was left of my hair. Without all my face-framing hair to signal to others, and myself, that I was a girl, my gender felt like it had become a clean slate from which I could craft an entirely new person. This possibility was both exhilarating and terrifying.

It felt freeing to shed my locks and unburden myself of all their time-sucking daily rituals. Shampooing, rinsing, conditioning, brushing, detangling, straightening, and blow-drying. Scrunching (if curly), and don't forget the appropriate curly-hair products or, if it was going to be straight, blow-drying with one of those godforsaken round blow-dryer brushes I could never get the hang of. The effort didn't seem worth it anymore. People at college seemed to like my new hair too.

"Laila told me she loved your new haircut," Ashley said to me one afternoon. She had just finished working a shift at the front desk of the women's and gender studies department, where she was a student worker. "She said that now your beauty is able to shine through even more."

Hearing that compliment from Laila, someone whom I admired dearly because of the powerful way in which she intertwined her scholarship and activism on behalf of women in the Middle East with her passion for the performing arts, made me feel like I was walking on a cloud as I strolled beside Ashley in the quad. It was a beautiful autumn day in the city; the leaves were just beginning to change, and a few twirled in the air on their way to the ground.

Ashley and I climbed up onto a grassy hill overlooking the quad and lay down beside one another. With my hand in hers, I exhaled.

"I told my mom," I said.

"Yikes. What did Laurie say?" Ashley asked, referring to my mother.

"Well, at first she was just, like, 'No, you didn't; stop lying to me, Jen.' But when she realized I wasn't playing, she was all, like, 'Why are you doing this to me?'"

"Oh jeez, your mother is hilarious. Did she cry?"

"No, but she told me she was going to kick my ass when she saw me."

"She's not gonna kick your ass," Ashley reassured me.

"I know, but she also said my grandma is going to have a heart attack and that my dad is going to kill me."

"She's not being serious, though, boo."

"Yes, she is," I said, rubbing my hand back and forth over my head, which had transitioned from feeling like Velcro to feeling like velvet. "Remember when I got my tattoo?" I asked. I had gotten my first tattoo a few months before—an equal sign on the back of my neck. When I had gone home for the weekend to do laundry, my father had shown up at my mom's front door to drop something off and noticed I was avoiding him. I answered the door when he rang the bell, and when I saw him, I quietly panicked. I tried walking backward to prevent him from seeing the back of my neck, and he noticed.

Before I could fully turn around and get away, he clenched me firmly with his strong grip.

"Get over here," he said between his teeth. "You think you're slick, huh?" He had fire in his eyes, and a grin spread across his face at the same time.

I was caught.

He took it pretty well, considering *I'll break your fuckin' legs* was one of his favorite ways to scare my sister and me away from getting tattoos. Actually, it was his go-to for scaring us away from pretty much anything he didn't approve of. My dad was always trying to protect us from everything with that veiled threat, whether it was riding on the back of some boy's fictitious motorcycle or, you know, the perilous dangers of going on a date before we turned thirty-five.

I shuddered to think what his response would be to *Hi, Dad, just checking in to let you know I shaved my head. And oh, by the way, I'm a lesbian now.*

I opted to not dwell on the possibilities.

I saw my mother that weekend. At first, she put on a big shocked face. She kept repeating the same phrase: "I can't believe you did this to me." But she eventually cooled down. After all, it was less permanent than a tattoo.

My gram wasn't as quick to accept my new look. Gram had recently been diagnosed with dementia and had moved in with my mom and

Bobby. Part of Gram's journey with the disease was the gradual dissipation of her social filter. I heard her before I saw her.

"Yoo-hoo." Her trademark greeting echoed in the corridor as she descended the two flights of shiny wooden stairs. Her hair was flat in the back, and her usually pristine magenta gel-tipped nails had grown out a bit, showing new, unpainted growth. But other than that, I was relieved to see that not much had changed since she was diagnosed.

When she finally saw me, she let out a gasp.

"What the *hell* did you do that for? Are you crazy? What is wrong with you? WHAT IS WRONG WITH YOU? Lord, please forgive my crazy granddaughter! And please forgive this crazy family of mine. This family is nuts, Lord. Nuts! You're all nuts, I tell ya!"

"So you like it?" I asked cheekily.

"No! For being a smart kid, you're pretty stupid sometimes. For God's sake!"

"I love you too," I said before giving her a big hug and kissing her on the cheek.

"When you fall asleep tonight, I'm gonna string you up by your feet and shave your armpits," she threatened me. Then she sighed. "Why can't you just be normal?" Her question jolted me. It came from a loving place of wanting to protect me, but it was one I had finally stopped asking myself. Performing normal was no longer the only path to happiness.

In the undergraduate WGS program, I met so many new people. Both FIA! and my classes were full of like-minded people who became part of my community, and some, such as Flowers and H, even became like family. It was in these classes that I found the comfort and safety to speak about my intersex experience in front of a small group of people.

WGS was the impetus for so many firsts in my life, like performing on a stage for *The Vagina Monologues* and learning about organizing and experiencing my first protests. This kind of engaged community—people who challenged the status quo when it came to binary ways of thinking—was the thing that had been missing from my life. I had finally found my people.

Everything was changing so quickly. I no longer considered myself female or a woman. But I didn't feel like I was male or a man either. I just felt intersex. I felt like me. And I was no longer so invested in figuring out what my gender was. But I did feel like I needed to really show the ways I'd changed. The tattoo, the haircut, the wardrobe shifts—those were all parts of claiming my new identity. I had to try on new things to find what fit; I had to let go of this mask of femininity that I'd been clinging to so tightly throughout junior high and high school.

I also began experimenting with a new name to reflect my growth. I wanted to find a name that was cute, different, and genderless. I wanted a name that felt like me, and I kept thinking about the pigeon that had wandered onto the bus that day. It seemed so independent, so free. It didn't care what anyone thought of it. It didn't care if it wasn't allowed on the bus. It had wings, and it could fly, and that's all that mattered. For the first time in my life, I felt like I had wings. Like I could fly.

So, on a whim, I changed my name on Facebook to Pidgeon. I put a *d* before the *g* in the name because I thought it looked better that way. The new name stuck. My college friends started calling me Pidgeon, or Pidge, and my childhood dream of having a nickname finally came true. Since claiming this new, non-gendered name for myself, many people, mostly pigeon haters, started asking me, "Why in the world would you name yourself that? You know we call them rats with wings?"

"Why not?" I'd shrug before confounding them by listing all of the amazing attributes I had recently discovered belonged to my fearless feathered brethren.

PART III

CHAPTER 11

Before WGS majors could graduate, we each had to complete a thesis research project and present our findings to a room full of people. We were encouraged to invite our families and close friends. I invited everyone in my family and Flowers, the person with the gentle expression and big brown eyes whom I had met at FIA! To my surprise, almost all my family members came, including both of my parents; my stepparents; my siblings, Nicole and Tommy; and both grandmothers—Gram and my yiayia.

I stood there a different person. Short hair. A tattoo. Nose ring. I no longer looked like the Trinity graduate my family had sent off to college. I no longer looked like a run-of-the-mill Elmwood Park girl who more or less blended in with most of the other girls. I no longer cared about looking like a normal girl—whatever that means. For my family, it was a big shift to see me like this, but they didn't let that get in the way of supporting me at this moment. Despite any disagreements they had with some of the choices I had made, they were able to look past that and be proud of me. They had come that day to show their support. It felt like I was playing softball, and they were all in the stands to cheer me on.

By this point, I had broken up with Ashley—who was also presenting their thesis that afternoon—but we'd managed to stay friends. The event was like a merging of my old and new lives, my blood family on one side—my roots—and my chosen family on the other.

As I looked out into the audience with my notes in my hand, I was terrified.

I called my thesis "Reclaiming the Gaze: From the Medical Establishment Back to the Intersex." I had interviewed intersex activists in the Bay Area, including the founder of the Intersex Society of North America, Bo Laurent, and others in Chicago, including Lynnell. I had also woven my own narrative into my research findings. And I had prepared a fiery, no-holds-barred presentation.

But practicing in front of WGS professors and students was a whole other thing than actually delivering this thesis—which so intimately announced my evolving views and declared my painful experience—in front of my family. Especially my devout, churchgoing grandmothers, whom I always strived to make proud.

When it was finally my turn to give my eight-minute presentation, my adrenaline kicked into high gear. I wondered, again, if I was going to pass out. I felt like I couldn't get enough oxygen into my lungs. Everything took on a surreal aura.

I took a deep, deep breath, and I began. I came out swinging.

"When I was a year and a half old, my vagina became a source of anxiety for the adults in my life," I said.

I watched my mother's eyes grow wide. I saw my gram cock her head. I noticed my professor Laila Farah squint her eyes and nod once, as if to say, *You got this.* I continued. I hadn't warned anyone about the topic of my thesis. There had been no way for them to prepare for what was about to happen.

"A few weeks later, it was determined by a team of experts at a local children's hospital who had been compiled to manage bodies like mine, bodies that refused to fit into their categories, that my undescended testes needed to be removed."

I could feel the tears welling in my eyes. I had wanted so badly to be strong, to get through the entire speech without crying. But there I was, feeling the burning redness of my heartbreak pooling in my eyes and then dripping down my cheeks.

"When presented with an opportunity to do original research for my thesis, I immediately knew what I wanted to do. After reading the literature currently available on the topic of intersexuality, it became clear to me that not only is there a lack of intersex voices, but there are even fewer accounts of intersexed people engaging in dialogue with one another."

At this point, I could feel myself getting stronger. I needed to do this, to get these words unstuck from my throat and out into the world. I had not spoken about my experience in depth to anyone in my family besides my mother. None of them were primed to hear the truth about what I'd been through.

I powered on.

"The medical establishment has traditionally had the privilege of interpreting our experiences, and, as a result, our voices have been marginalized. I chose to address the ways in which the medical establishment has violated the positive construction of intersex identities. My research aims to challenge *their* assumptions about *our* bodies, and works to place the lived experiences of intersex people at the center of analysis."

The speech continued for what felt like a lifetime but was only a handful of minutes. By the time I got to the last page, my hands were sweating, my throat was dry, and my face was red. But I felt empowered and alive in a way I never had.

"I would like to close with the following thoughts on what it means when we pardon our doctors, as two of the participants did in the interviews I conducted, and as I am repeatedly expected to do. When we say we don't think the doctors *meant* to hurt us and we pardon them as uneducated or at worst ignorant, we are again rendered silent. Whether they *meant* to hurt us or not does not take away from the fact that they have, currently are, and will continue to hurt us. No matter how much my doctors smiled and cracked jokes with me during my annual checkups, they were still the same men who decided it was best to permanently disfigure my body in the name of normality.

"If we continue to pardon them, I fear we run the risk of normalizing *their* behavior. What happened to each of us individually cannot be isolated from what has happened to all of us. Whether we as intersex individuals want to acknowledge it, the doctors *are* part of our community. They have been responsible for fundamentally shifting the ways in which we react, and are reacted to, as gendered and sexed individuals.

"As one person shared, 'Ideally, they would become our allies,' and as another individual stated, as our allies they need to be aware that 'we need medical attention, but not to be medicalized. It's when we are medicalized, viewed as other or less than, that doctors' ethics and commitment to *first do no harm* seems to be conveniently forgotten.'

"The hermaphrodite is something not human, and it is in this imagined state that our bodies are fair game for the torture they pass off as medically necessary treatment. Our bodies do not fit into neat either/or categories. Since our bodies refuse to be categorized and named, violence is inflicted upon them to demand order out of our ambiguity. A culture that refuses to acknowledge our both/and status as legitimate is what needs fixing, not our bodies. When we dismiss what the doctors have done as anything other than sheer violence, we become complicit in a vendetta that systematically seeks to erase our identities because our bodies disrupt their binary belief system.

"As Cal Stephanides, the protagonist in *Middlesex*, said:

> I was beginning to understand something about normality. Normality wasn't normal. It couldn't be. If normality were normal, everybody could leave it alone. They could sit back and let normality manifest itself. But people— and especially doctors—had doubts about normality. They weren't sure normality was up to the job. And so they felt inclined to give it a boost."

After everyone was done with their presentations and the ceremony ended, a line of people, members of other students' families, started to form in front of me. I didn't understand what they wanted, and I darted my eyes around to see if my family was still there. Then one of the people standing in front of me, an older white gentleman who looked like he was someone's father, asked if he could shake my hand.

"Thank you so much for sharing your story," he said. "I never knew about what intersex people endured before today. You opened my eyes, and I just needed to come up and say thank you."

I was shocked. I couldn't believe that a stranger, someone who looked like your average straight white guy from Middle America, was receptive to the rage-filled feminist fire I had just spit. Many other strangers came up and did the same, and as they approached me, I could see my family, every single one of them, waiting in line behind them.

When my family hugged me and told me what a good job I had done, and how proud they were of me, I started to cry. It was then I realized that my yiayia, whose reaction I feared the most, probably wasn't upset with me, even though she was the most old-school member of my family. She smiled and hugged me and kissed me on the cheek. "I'm so proud of you, sweetheart," she told me. As she left the presentation, clutching my father's arm, she asked in Greek: "Τι σημαίνει ο ερμαφρόδιτος"—English translation: "What's a hermaphrodite?"

After my presentation, my mother approached and gave me a hug. I wondered if she felt a bit embarrassed by what I had shared. She always felt that private matters should be kept inside the family. But she smiled and congratulated me. She said, "I'm very proud of you, *Pidgeon*."

She emphasized my new name, signaling that it was both difficult for her to do and that she was trying. I think it was the first time she called me by my new name. I let her words hang in the air a bit.

And then, on the inside, I felt like I was running, two wings ripping through my shoulder blades, spreading wide, and lifting me up.

CHAPTER 12

After I graduated, I was determined to make a difference in my community. I had just delivered my thesis and felt the type of fresh idealism that can come from living your truth and finding a community that accepts and celebrates you.

About four years later, I decided to continue my education as a graduate student studying intersexuality and health communication at DePaul in the women's and gender studies program.

The years between college and grad school had been filled with relationships with women that ultimately ended but forced me to consider things I'd never had the chance to think about before: concepts of boundaries and healthy love. To pay the bills, I worked grinding jobs at coffee shops and retail stores, car dealerships and fine-dining restaurants. I was a wedding photographer and interned at a video production house. I was trying on jobs and seeing how they fit. And during this time, I began to land gigs as a speaker educating the public about the intersex community. At first, the speaking jobs didn't pay all that much. They came few and far between. But I could see there was a need for this work, a hunger.

Throughout all that time, the one consistent job I had was working as an assistant for a retired WGS professor and executive director of her family's charitable trust. Dr. Irene Beck and her partner, Bill Beck, a retired finance expert and now president of the same trust, gave me more than just a job—it was a mentorship. In the four years between college and grad school, Irene and Bill became like surrogate parents to me. And it was Irene who first floated the idea of grad school. I wanted to continue to fight for the intersex community. To act as a shield between vulnerable kids and the doctors who threaten to hurt them. I dreamed of becoming a professor, or starting my own nonprofit. But I didn't have a road map. I didn't know how to get to the next step. So when Irene suggested that perhaps I should continue my education, it turned my aimlessness into action.

At the onset of most of my new graduate classes, the professors would begin with a check-in, which included us sharing our gender pronouns—just like at FIA! meetings. But now I was a bit more familiar with the concept and had started thinking about using they/them as my own pronouns. But I wasn't quite sure yet. So when my turn to check in came, I would say "she/her and . . . they/them" as a way to test out the waters. Eventually, I dropped the she/her for they/them, because just she/her stopped seeming appropriate for my intersex body, my body that refused to be either/or.

In that first year of grad school, we were required to take an internship course. Irene thought it would be a good idea to pitch myself as an intern to the team at Lurie Children's Hospital, where I could work with intersex kids in the new Sex Development Clinic. When I contacted the hospital, they gave me a meeting with Dr. Frader, who was the Sex Development Clinic's bioethicist. During our meeting, I handed him my proposal, which laid out all the labor I'd be willing to do for the clinic as a grad student and former patient.

The proposal, which Irene helped me craft and print out, sat on Dr. Frader's desk. It included the usual intern-type things a grad student might offer, like helping them out with their social media presence and creating brochures for their waiting room. But I had an ulterior motive. I wanted to throw a wrench in their machine—the one that attempted to de-intersex kids who were born like me. I thought if I could volunteer my time as a community liaison and share my experiences, I could support parents and kids on the cusp of going through something similar. I had hoped to be their local on-call intersex patient advocate. I wanted to offer myself as a pit stop between the clinic and the operating room.

"I am offering you all of this for free," I said.

How could they pass this up? I thought. A former intersex patient of theirs was offering free labor as a graduate student from a nearby university. I thought they would see it as an incredible opportunity.

At the end of my meeting with Dr. Frader, we shook hands. I noticed a ring on his finger with a rainbow on it. I interpreted the ring as a signal to mean we might have a shared vision and, hopefully, a mutual goal. Learning that there was at least one fellow queer person working at this institution, in the actual clinic that saw intersex kids, brought a tepid sense of relief to me. *Maybe they'll say yes?*

"Thanks for coming by," he said. "I'll run this by the others on the team, and we'll be in touch."

No one ever got back to me.

* * *

Some months later, I moved into a new apartment in Chicago, on the city's far North Side in a neighborhood called Rogers Park, with roommates I had met after posting an ad on Craigslist. The first was Maricarmen, one of the most beautiful women I had ever seen. She was from Mexico City. She had moved to Chicago to study art direction in a two-year program at a school downtown. After meeting her on Skype for just a few moments, I developed an instant crush on her long eyelashes and sweet demeanor. She could have told me that she never did her dishes and had a pet Komodo dragon and it wouldn't have mattered one bit. I was as crushed out as you can be over someone you just met seconds before on Skype, and I quickly let her know the room was hers if she wanted it. The third room was occupied by a queer couple, two women in their midtwenties from Seattle, whom I also met online. They were moving to the city as well—one was going to study social work as a grad student at the University of Chicago, and the other was coming along to support her as a partner.

Our new apartment was on the second floor of a sturdy red-brick three-flat owned by a lesbian couple in their midforties. It was nestled in the middle of a lush, tree-lined side street. It was a gorgeous three-bedroom with hardwood floors and a dreamy sunroom that was engulfed by the leaves of the trees. Even though most of the apartment's original character was hidden under thick layers of stark-white paint, it was still one of the most handsome places I had ever lived in. It even had one of those nonfunctional but still beautiful fireplaces tucked between a pair of built-in bookshelves.

After the four of us—actually five if you counted Callie, my recently adopted rottweiler—got settled in, we all quickly embarked on the next chapters of our lives.

I was juggling class and a job as a graduate assistant overseeing a teen dating violence prevention program—Take Back the Halls, or TBTH. The program was held after school in the Chicago Public High School system. I had been an intern in the program as an undergrad, and now, in grad school, I had secured an assistantship position overseeing the undergrad interns across multiple high schools. It was work I believed in, and it helped me pay my grad school tuition. We aimed to give students tools to navigate their dating relationships in healthier ways. I wished I'd had TBTH myself in high school, when I was struggling through the turbulence with Mike. That may have been why I kept returning to the job, year after year: to help students who were enduring similar turmoil in their dating relationships.

That same year, I also began working for Advocates for Informed Choice, or AIC for short, a legal nonprofit that fought to protect the rights of intersex youth.

AIC was the only nonprofit in the United States that was solely dedicated to protecting the legal rights of intersex people. Part of their strategy was training the next generation of intersex activists by creating an intersex youth advocacy group called Inter/Act.

I was the youth leadership coordinator and the operations manager. At first, I was corralling a small group of mostly anonymous intersex youth, making sure they submitted weekly writing entries about their experiences for our Tumblr blog. This task was one I inherited from our former coordinator, Jim Ambrose.

But soon after I started in my new role, our young cohort began to grow, and so did my responsibilities.

Quickly my tasks at work shifted and became less about blog posts and more about planning the first ever intersex youth retreat in Northern California. Coincidentally, it was going to be held at the same location where the first ever intersex retreat organized by ISNA was held in 1996. There was no denying the work I was helping to accomplish was important. Yet wearing so many hats, all at once, was both exhilarating and exhausting.

I said yes to the position at AIC not only because it was aligned with my values and goals but also because it would allow me to pay my rent. I was drop-dead tired most nights, and sometimes days, but for the first time in my life, my work and my purpose were intersecting.

I was feeling proud of myself.

Around this time, I got a call from my friend Mika, who was excited about interviewing me for StoryCorps, a nonprofit organization. Their mission is to record, preserve, and share the stories of Americans from diverse backgrounds. Mika asked if I'd come down to one of their recording studios and talk with her about my family's history.

I agreed.

But I had no idea this one simple conversation with a friend would end up sparking a war with part of the American medical community. That war would consume years of my life and lead me straight back to the steps of my childhood hospital. I had no idea, as I walked downtown and into that soundproofed studio in a converted Airstream trailer, that I was about to fire the first shot and become one of the faces of the intersex movement worldwide.

The conversation with Mika began innocently. She asked me about my family's origins in Chicago, and I shared some snippets of stories I'd been collecting throughout the years. Like the story of my great-grandfather being killed by Nazis when they attempted to occupy Athens. And the one about my grandma as a child playing Kick the Can on Artesian Avenue in Chicago during the Great Depression. I also spoke about the brutal mafia-ordered murder of my uncle and about how his tragic death led to an unraveling that my mom's family never quite healed from.

As we were nearing the end of our hour, Mika asked me one last question. A question I wasn't prepared for. The question that would change everything.

"Pidgeon, I was wondering if in the little time we have left, you could share a little bit about your story? About growing up intersex and your fight to make things better for other intersex kids?"

I hadn't been expecting the question but decided I was game.

Then I took a deep breath, and in the last ten minutes or so, I told my intersex story. I took her through the inhumane surgeries I'd endured, the awful advice the doctors at Lurie told my parents and me. I told her about the castration and the other violating surgeries and how they still go on today, all over the country—and the world. I opened the floodgates, and it all came pouring out of me. I figured nobody would ever hear my interview. I figured I was talking to an audience of one.

I was wrong.

A few weeks after I recorded the StoryCorps interview, I received a call from an NPR producer. They said they wanted to use part of my interview on WBEZ, our local NPR affiliate in Chicago. My story would be broadcast to my community. The section they wanted to use was about my intersex experience.

After the segment aired on WBEZ, things felt a little out of control. I was inundated with interview requests from the media, who wanted to know more about my experiences as an intersex person.

I was a bit rattled by this new wave of attention, but I tried my best to never pass up an opportunity to speak out. I was determined to do anything I could to let people know what was going on behind closed doors at beloved children's hospitals like Lurie. I wanted to bring awareness that could end the harmful practices done to intersex people.

In those years since I discovered the truth about what happened to me, I'd transformed in so many ways. I'd stopped pouring all my energy into fitting the narrow mold of femininity and refocused myself and my time. I became fully fixated on ending intersex surgeries. It had become more than just a goal; it had become an obsession. The more time I spent around other intersex people, especially those who were advocating for our rights to be recognized, the more I felt determined to fight for this change. I attended support groups where I met intersex people and families who had experiences similar to mine. Their stories fueled me.

The story attracted more than just media attention—it also attracted the attention of Lurie. One day, not long after the radio segment aired, I came home to a panicked voice mail.

"Hi, this message is for Pidgeon. This is Julie from Lurie Children's Hospital. We heard your story on WBEZ and would like to discuss your comments. Please call us back as soon as you can. Thank you."

Apparently, Lurie had heard my little interview. They were not pleased.

Hearing her message gave me an exhilarating sense of power—one that both excited and unnerved me. I felt like I was finally making some headway but also like I was in trouble, like I used to feel when I was about to be grounded. I immediately looked Julie up on the internet. Her LinkedIn profile described her job duties as "Media Relations, Crisis Communications, Public Affairs." The crisis communications part stood out.

After the message from Lurie, I felt I needed some advice on how to seize this opportunity. I knew just who to call. The founder of Advocates for Informed Choice, my boss, was a whip-smart attorney named Anne Tamar-Mattis who lived in Northern California. Anne had become a trusted mentor to me in the short time I had been working at her nonprofit. She wasn't intersex, but she was married to an intersex person—one who also happened to be both an intersex advocate and a physician. I had become acquainted with the two of them over the years attending support group meetings—and now I worked for Anne.

"Anne," I said. "You'll never believe who just called me."

"Who?"

"Lurie Children's Hospital!"

Anne was up to speed on the radio interview, thanks to our weekly check-ins for work.

"Wow," Anne said. "What did they say?"

"They called me twice. Yesterday the PR people left a message. Today it was someone who said she worked with actual intersex kids in their clinic. She wants to, like, set up a call or something."

"That's intense," Anne said. "How are you doing?"

"I'm just trying to figure out how to respond. I don't know what's the best next move here, you know?" I still felt burned by my earlier meeting with the Sex Development Clinic. When I wanted to help by interning for them, they had ignored me. It was hard to imagine that they were reaching out with pure intentions.

"How can I support you?" Anne was always so supportive. She was a rock for me and so many other intersex people whenever we had strategy questions. Her calm demeanor, which never seemed to falter, helped soothe those of us who turned to her for help. She was like an aunt whom all of us intersex activists and advocates could call for advice, or just a nudge.

"I think right now I just need you to tell me what you think is the best next step."

"That depends on your goals."

It was a question I'd considered but hadn't articulated. "My goal is to get them to end the surgeries."

"Right." She paused. "Then I think a good next step might be to call that person from the clinic back and talk to her. You can get a feel for what she wants and see if you feel comfortable asking to set up a meeting with them."

I was nervous but nodding. What she was saying made sense. But it wasn't easy for me to trust people who worked at the site where my body had been repeatedly pillaged while I was a patient of theirs.

The doctors at Lurie had lied to me for close to eighteen years of my life. They had ignored my proposal to intern for them. Yet now, because a tiny bit of my story had found its way onto public radio, I was supposed to believe they suddenly cared about me? I had been traumatized and abused by this institution. They had spent years gaslighting me, manipulating me with lies. And I was still dealing with the effects of that trauma and physical harm. This was the place that tried to deny my body the right to exist. And now they were saying that they wanted to talk to me. My this-is-a-trap radar was going off.

"You don't have to," Anne said. "It's completely up to you. I can only imagine how triggering it could be for you to be in contact with them. But if you decide to go through with this, I will be here to support you however I can."

"Okay, Anne, thank you so much." I felt like I was on autopilot, like it was my duty to push forward, no matter the emotional toll. "I'll call her back and let her know that I want to set up a meeting."

"Don't forget," Anne said. "I'm here."

⚘

The next day, I spoke with Jen Leininger, the Sex Development Clinic coordinator at Lurie. Jen offered to schedule a meeting with me, herself, and the man who ran the clinic—a pediatric urologist named Dr. Earl Cheng.

During that initial conversation, Jen was friendly and apologized for the call I received from Julie in the PR department. She explained that Julie's department had panicked a bit when they heard my radio piece, and that they shouldn't have called me like that.

"Our team is committed to doing everything we can to improve the experiences of our intersex patients," Jen said. "The reason I reached out is to see if you'd be willing to sit down with us so we can hear about your experience, and possibly answer any questions you might have, and hopefully figure out if there's any support that our team can offer to you."

Oh, now they want to talk to me.

I didn't know what to make of her proposal.

I was conflicted.

On the one hand, I was on high alert. There was nothing in my past that made me want to revisit Lurie, especially now that it didn't feel like a visit would be on my terms. I didn't trust Jen or anyone else who worked at the clinic. On the other hand, I decided my end goal was more important. Ending the surgeries was beyond necessary. Maybe this could help. I agreed to enter the belly of the beast.

"Sure," I said in a deadpan tone.

Perhaps I was foolish to say yes so quickly. Perhaps I was suffering from a bit of Stockholm syndrome, and it made me eager to try and work alongside the same surgeons who'd scarred me in the first place. Or perhaps I was just younger and more optimistic. Maybe even naive. I wanted to believe that maybe, just maybe, these doctors were ready to confront face-to-face the devastation that they'd etched into my being.

It was probably a little bit of each of those reasons that compelled me to agree to return to the heartless hospital that had only recently, thanks to their policy of only *treating* children, discharged me. But more than anything, I agreed because ever since I found out the truth about what had happened to me, I felt compelled, as if it were a duty, to do what I could to prevent the same thing from happening to others.

I didn't want to do it. I had to.

As soon as I hung up with Jen, I called Anne. "Anne? Do you have a minute?"

"Sure, what's up?"

"I spoke with Lurie. They asked to have a meeting, and I said yes."

"Wow. Are you okay? How do you feel?"

"Nervous. Scared. Anxious."

"When do they want to meet?" she asked. "And where?"

"Downtown," I said. "In some underground train-station coffee shop near Millennium Park."

The weirdness of the location became more apparent as I said it out loud.

"And it's just going to be a meeting between you and the coordinator of the clinic?"

Anne's deposition skills were on full display.

"Her and Earl," I replied.

"Earl's going to be there?" She sounded concerned.

"Yeah, that's what Jen said." My tone said, *I'll see it when I believe it.*

"Okay, so these two people think they're going to intimidate you into shutting up in some basement in downtown Chicago?"

God, she was good.

"No way, I'm coming with you," she said in a tone of voice that told me she meant business.

"You're what? How are you going to do that? You live so far!"

"It just so happens that I have a deposition with a surgeon in Oklahoma the day after your meeting. If you'd like, I can fly to Chicago first and be there with you."

Everyone in the intersex world, especially physicians, knew who Anne was because she was currently in the process of suing the doctors who performed barbaric surgeries on babies in both federal and state courts.

"Oh my God, Anne, I would love it if you'd be there with me," I said. "I was so nervous to do this alone."

"You won't be alone," she said. "You're not alone."

❦

The goal of the meeting was simple. I wanted Dr. Earl Cheng to take public accountability for the harm he and his colleagues had done to intersex patients. I wanted them to agree to stop performing these inhumane surgeries on babies. I wanted to hear him say he would stop.

Admittedly, it wasn't a simple task. I knew we had a mountain to climb. And I hoped I was ready to climb it.

❦

When I saw Anne exit the Adams/Wabash station in the Loop, I immediately noticed she was wearing her court outfit—an unassuming pair of beige dress slacks and a matching blazer. Her hair was tied back in her trademark half ponytail. At first glance, Anne looked like a lovely, put-together lady, but underneath her demure facade was a radical and queer executive director who was gifted at trailblazing law practices. She was like my own personal Ruth Bader Ginsburg, one I could actually call up when I needed advice.

As we walked together to the meeting, we went over our last-minute game plan.

"I won't say anything unless you want me to," she said. "I know you're going to be great, but you can give me a look to let me know if you ever feel like you want me to jump in. But my goal is to be a support to you. I'm here to be here for you."

And then we began our descent into the underground train station where the meeting was going to be held inside a cramped, windowless Starbucks. We found a table near the front. Anne placed her briefcase on the table.

"It's to intimidate them," she said.

"For real?"

"There's nothing scarier to these people than seeing a lawyer with her briefcase sitting across the table from them."

I didn't know it was possible, but my admiration for Anne increased tenfold in that moment. She was such a boss. And I loved her for it.

The clock clicked closer to showtime.

As far as Jen and Earl knew, I was showing up alone. They didn't have any idea I was bringing Anne with me. I hadn't given them any warning. As a people pleaser, this tiny bit of duplicity was making me feel a bit more anxious than I would have felt had I told them.

And then I saw them coming. I took a deep breath.

Here we go.

I noticed Earl first. He was taller than I thought he'd be and a bit younger. He was balding but still had a youthful expression that seemed to suggest he couldn't hurt a fly. His clinic coordinator, Jen Leininger, walked a few paces behind him. She had blue eyes and straight blonde hair.

When Earl saw me, he got this look in his eye, like he was gleefully preparing to steal cake from a baby. Then he saw Anne and his jaw dropped. Suddenly, he looked less confident about his cake heist.

"And who is this?" he asked.

"Oh, hello. I'm Anne," she said. "Nice to meet you."

Earl and Jen just looked at her with blank expressions on their faces. Anne didn't skip a beat.

"Oh, forgive me, I forgot to mention, I'm the executive director at Advocates for Informed Choice. I work with Pidgeon. They told me about your meeting today, and I thought I'd come, too, to support my colleague."

Earl's blank stare was starting to foment into something else. He was clearly displeased with the situation that had just smacked him upside his head.

Then Anne put the nail in the coffin.

"It just so happened that I had a long layover in Chicago today on my way down to Oklahoma City, where I'll be conducting a deposition tomorrow. I think you might know him? He's one of your colleagues who works at the children's hospital down there."

I felt the tiniest of smirks form at the corner of my lip.

Anne was clearly in charge at this moment, and Jen and Earl had shrunk to a tenth of their former selves in a matter of seconds. I watched Anne's exquisite takedown with the glee of a Bulls fan who somehow won courtside playoff tickets in the '90s.

"Yes, I know him," Earl said as he cleared his throat. "He's an excellent surgeon."

Jen tried her best to keep her expression cordial, nodding and smiling at what she thought were appropriate times.

But Earl had steam coming out of his ears.

Witnessing the surgeon, who'd thought he'd have an easy job of stitching up my lips, squirm in his chair was an incredibly cathartic experience. For the first time, I was with these doctors as myself; I wasn't a passive patient or compliant child who was ignorant of being intersex. In this moment, I was a defiant intersex adult, emerging from a chrysalis anew.

"I'll be sure to let him know we met," Anne stoically replied.

The rest of our meeting was something of a train wreck.

Unhinged by Anne's unexpected presence, Earl rambled for what seemed like hours about his accolades in addition to the trials and tribulations he'd endured as a surgical student. He told us about the sacrifices he had made to get to where he was today.

"We had so many brutal, long shifts during rounds," he lamented.

But if he was trying to gain sympathy from us, it wasn't working. Before I met him, I learned about what he did to young intersex patients, and I didn't like him. I wanted to tell him off, tell him that I hated him and every other surgeon like him. I wanted to kick and spit and scream and throw shit. I wanted to let out all the pain I had bottled up inside and splay it across our coffee-stained table in the subterranean Starbucks for him to mop up. But instead, Anne and I had somehow begun taking on the role of sounding board for all his insecurities.

The final straw was when this man randomly, for who knows what reason, decided it would be a good idea to tell us how he considered himself a Twinkie.

"I'm yellow on the outside but white on the inside. Like a Twinkie."

I could tell from Anne's exhale, and from the way she readjusted her hand clasp, that she thought this conversation was as bananas as I did.

"Thank you for sharing all of that with us, Earl," Anne said. "It was really . . . quite vulnerable."

When Jen had initially reached out to set up this meeting, she'd said it was because she wanted to hear from me and see if there was any way the clinic could offer support. But it was becoming obvious that, regardless of her intentions, Earl had a different agenda. It seemed he was only interested in hearing himself speak.

"Earlier in the conversation, you mentioned to Pidgeon and me that you wanted to be the one in your field to do better by intersex patients," Anne continued with a perfectly calculated jab.

"Yes, I do." Earl looked suspicious.

"To do that, you would have to be publicly accountable for the harm you and your profession have caused intersex people over the decades. Are you willing to do that?"

Anne landed her uppercut, and I was up on both feet cheering her on from the crowd.

Earl paused.

His eyes darted back and forth. He shifted in his seat as a bead of perspiration trickled down his forehead.

His sense of bravado was deflated.

"No," he said. "I'm not able to do that."

"Well, what *can* you do?" I asked.

"What do you want?" he asked as he shook his head and brought his shoulders closer to his ears.

"I want you and your entire staff to agree to stop performing surgeries on babies."

He didn't even take a beat before giving his answer.

"I can't do that," he said.

I had expected him to say no, but I also had a tiny reserve of hope that maybe, just maybe, he'd realize his wrongdoing. I thought maybe he'd want to fix the mess that he was responsible for perpetuating at Lurie ever since intersex patient care was centralized under his command. But Anne and I had prepared for this, and I had a counter-offer lined up and ready to go.

"Okay, well, that's disappointing," I said. "Would you be willing to allow the intersex group of young people I work with, Inter/Act, to come and give you and your colleagues at your clinic a training?"

Earl looked at Jen, his clinic coordinator, and she signaled that she was in agreement with a nod.

"I don't see why not," Earl replied. "Jen will be in touch to set up a date."

The rest of the meeting was a blur. There were some formalities at the end, the usual "thank you" and "appreciate you taking the time." When Anne and I finally reemerged to street level, we looked at each other and just shook our heads.

"What was that, Anne?" I couldn't hold it in anymore.

"That was rough," she replied. "How are you doing?"

"I'm okay," I said. "But oh my God, Anne, what in the actual fuck was that?"

"Surgeons are very . . . unique," Anne said. "But you were great, Pidgeon."

"Thanks, Anne. So were you!" I said, and I meant it.

We spent a couple of minutes rehashing the meeting with each other as commuters walked past us.

"When we check in next week on Monday, let's take some time to come up with a plan for your upcoming training."

The day finally came to give the training to Lurie's sex and gender clinic, and one of the young people in Inter/Act drove all the way from Michigan—about four hours from Chicago—to co-facilitate the presentation we had prepared.

We ended up sitting in an empty conference room for just over an hour, staring at each other in disbelief. They didn't even show up. We couldn't believe the disrespect. Just as we were about to give up and go home, Earl and his colleagues walked in the door.

"Sorry, got tied up in the clinic," he said as he and the others filed in and began taking seats.

I was irritated with their callousness, but I felt like I needed to keep it professional, since I was wearing my youth coordinator hat and one of Inter/Act's young members was present. I tried my best to keep everything cordial.

"Emily, do you have time to still give the presentation with me?" I asked.

She looked at her watch and decided that even though she'd be late returning home, it would be worth it—she hoped—to stay.

"Let's do it," she said.

With the little time we had left, Emily and I gave our presentation. Instead of focusing on the negative aspects of intersex bodies and using pathological terms to describe our body parts, like I assumed the doctors were used to, we focused on what made us unique and proud to be who we were. We talked about how our young members, of which we had fifteen or so at the time, all agreed that early interventions, especially those in the form of nonconsensual genital and reproductive organ surgeries, needed to end. We discussed how they brought nothing but pain to intersex people's lives. We underscored how bodily autonomy, not medical paternalism, was what intersex kids needed.

After our time was up, we left their meeting room and parted ways. I was proud of the work we had done but unsure of whether it would have the effect we wanted: getting Lurie to become the first hospital in the country to end surgeries on intersex kids. I walked out of the building deflated, with a sense of despair that nothing would change. I was so tired of playing their games. Asking to be their intern. Meeting with them and asking them to be accountable. Almost being stood up for our training. Meanwhile, more babies and kids were being mutilated at the hands of these surgeons. More people were being lied to. More surgeries were happening.

After the training, AIC reached out many more times to Lurie in the hopes of creating positive change for intersex kids, but nothing ever ultimately worked. Nothing really changed at Lurie. It was still business as usual in their Sex Development Clinic. Intersex kids' bodies were still being treated just as disposably in those years as they had been twenty-some years before, when I was born and growing up. Intersex kids who were seen at Lurie, and at every hospital around the country, were still being treated like pets who had no say over whether their reproductive organs would stay put. We were still undergoing *cosmetic procedures* that weren't much different from genital mutilation. We still had no power over our own destinies.

In the years after our dead-end attempts at working with Lurie, AIC and our young people in Inter/Act pushed forward. AIC's main objective in those years was the #Justice4MC case, a landmark medical malpractice lawsuit on behalf of an adopted intersex child in South Carolina who was publicly identified by only their initials, MC. Their operations—procedures meant to make them appear more like a *normal* female, much like the ones performed on me as a child—occurred before they were adopted, while they were under the state's care.

I was proud that the organization I worked for was working hard on this first-of-its-kind legal pursuit against those who had harmed MC. While the *treatments* they gave MC and me were almost identical, the time span between when they happened and when our parents found out was not. MC's adoptive parents, unlike mine, were aware of the intersex rights movement. After adopting their child, they reached out to AIC for help, and thankfully the statute of limitations hadn't yet expired. The case was a long uphill battle, but I hoped for MC—and maybe a little bit for my younger self as well—that they would get the justice they deserved.

At some point in early 2015, BuzzFeed contacted AIC in regard to our youth program, Inter/Act, of which I was the coordinator. They had hoped to collaborate with us on creating an informative video to help their viewers understand intersexuality better. After a few calls and some prep with their producers, I flew to Los Angeles to meet up with three others—Saifa, Emily, and Alice—who would be in the video as well. All four of us were intersex advocates and connected to AIC and Inter/Act in some way or another. Together we had lunch and met with the BuzzFeed producers in person to go over the rundown of our upcoming shoot.

This was huge. At the time, it seemed everyone was watching and sharing BuzzFeed's videos on social media. We knew this level of visibility had the potential to create a big cultural shift in terms of how we as intersex people were viewed and understood. And maybe, I hoped, it could even somehow help in the outcome of MC's case. After we shot it, the editors did their thing and released it on their YouTube channel under the title "What It's Like to Be Intersex."

Within days, the video had racked up hundreds of thousands of views, and by the end of the week, we were closing in on a million. A month later, we were well beyond that number. The three-minute-and-twenty-five-second video went viral. The cherry on top was that it wasn't a sensational piece that presented intersex people as broken and in need of fixing. Instead, this wide-reaching piece of content about our community was curated distinctly from the perspectives of four people who were all not only intersex but also young, queer, multicultural, and decidedly anti-surgery and pro–bodily autonomy.

We gave viewers intersex knowledge in a way that managed to be both heavy and lighthearted at once. During rehearsal, I'd pitched an idea to have one of us say on camera: "Raise your hands if you have testes." Then Emily—the person who appeared the most femme among us—would raise their hand, because they were the only one who still had their testes intact. Everyone seemed to like the idea, and the producers gave us the green light. The editors chose to use the clip to open the video.

In the video, Emily has long, flowy chestnut hair and big blue eyes, and wears a salmon-pink dress. The moment when they are the only person raising their hand challenges viewers' assumptions about what constitutes sex and gender. After their expectations are rattled, the rest of the video juxtaposes clips of us speaking about parts of our stories against answers to questions such as: *What should be done when an intersex kid is born?* Answer: *Leave them alone and love them.* The video introduced the binary-defying world of intersex people to the masses.

It was exhilarating to see those viewership numbers on the video go up. It was common to find out that organizations, companies, and schools were using the video as educational content in their diversity training. My sister, Nicole, even FaceTimed me once while training for a new job as a medical assistant in California, where she had recently moved, to show me that she was watching the video alongside her fellow new hires.

You're famous sis, she texted.

Ha, yeah right, I replied.

While none of us in the video were famous, the video's reach was wild. There were hundreds, if not thousands, of comments from people all across the globe telling us how much the video had made an impact on them. If they weren't intersex, they were happy to learn about the topic. If they were intersex themselves, they were grateful to feel seen in a way that wasn't the usual pathological way. The video helped so many of us intersex people feel a bit more validated and understood.

It was then I realized the sheer power embedded in media. Especially social media. It became clear to me that it was an underutilized tool in our community that we could use to coordinate our efforts and help spread the word that intersex surgeries, and all the other harm doctors forced us to undergo, needed to end.

A few months after the success of our BuzzFeed video, I received an email from Associated Press reporter Lindsey Tanner requesting an interview. According to her email, she was writing a story about intersex people and recent changes, spurred by pressure from intersex activism, at sites such as Lurie's Sex Development Clinic.

She explained that they wanted to interview someone like me, someone who had been a patient at the hospital before the new, ostensibly more progressive interdisciplinary clinic had launched.

"I have also reached out to the head of the Sex Development Clinic at Lurie, Dr. Earl Cheng, and I'm hoping to interview him as well."

Earl and I were to meet again, except this time in print.

It was my first time receiving a request from a major global news organization. They were also interviewing doctors at Lurie about the supposed positive changes, but that was odd, given that they were still doing surgeries, albeit more *conscientiously*. Lurie billed its darling of a new clinic, which had launched in 2013, as being "interdisciplinary" and having a "patient-centered" approach to intersex care. Its stakeholders—namely Earl and a few of his colleagues—seemed determined to get the word out about their shiny new *progressive* program. The truth of the matter was that not much had changed at Lurie when it came to intersex patients. Instead of seeing different doctors on different days, patients got to see them all at once on specially designated clinic days. The clinic was promoted as some great step forward, but to me, it was just a glossy reformulation of the same old methods they'd always used to harm kids like me. New clinic or not, Lurie was still denying intersex people their bodily autonomy and performing medically unnecessary and oftentimes mutilative surgeries that left behind nerve damage and scar tissue. What had changed, though, as evidenced in part by the request from the AP to write such an article, was the amount of scrutiny hospitals like Lurie were now under. For the first time, it seemed they were feeling enough pressure—thanks, in large part, to the efforts of AIC, Inter/Act, and other similar organizations in the US and around the world—to actually try and *appear* to be doing better. Despite the face-lift, its soul hadn't changed.

I knew Earl would gloat about how great their new clinic was and how they weren't *as bad* as they were in the *old days*, but still I said yes to the interview. I decided the benefits of getting an intersex story such as mine out there to an audience—many of whom BuzzFeed wouldn't reach—outweighed the cons of being in a story that included Lurie's finely woven publicity stunts.

A few weeks later, on April 17, 2015, I woke up to discover the AP article, titled "Intersex Surgeries Spark Move Away from Drastic Treatment," had gone out over the wire and been picked up by national and international news outlets. I went online and began reading:

> Pagonis' parents knew nothing about the conditions—or about the surgeries' troubling risks, including damage to sexual functioning, satisfaction and psyche later on.

> Now, efforts are underway to change the way intersex children are treated . . .

> The program is one of several nationwide that employ a team of specialists including surgeons, hormone experts, genetic counselors, psychologists and ethicists.

The team helps families weigh their options, including whether surgery should be considered at all.

"The way that we took care of things in the past . . . where there was a fair amount of secrecy, where there was surgery done in the infant state, and potentially irreversible surgery, is probably not the best way to go about things," said Dr. Earl Cheng.

After the AP article came out, I was increasingly frustrated with Earl's ability to obfuscate the truth of what was still happening at his clinic. The spotlight from the article had put some cool things into motion, including an award from the Obama White House for my advocacy work. I was invited to receive it at the White House, where I met Joey Soloway. Being that we were both from Chicago, we hit it off immediately. At the end of the evening, I floated an idea to Joey: that he should put an intersex character in his show (wink, wink). Shortly after, I received an email telling me that *Transparent* had written in an intersex character named Baxter who was based on me, and Joey wanted me to come to Hollywood to film it. It was a dream experience to be on the set of an award-winning show alongside one of the best directors in the business. But I couldn't shake the fact that even with all this press and exposure, no real change was happening with Lurie and Earl. It was infuriating. Even the UN had taken a strong public stance against intersex surgeries in 2013, categorizing them as forms of torture. Yet no institutions in the US, let alone clinics like Lurie, were taking action. After reading the article, something shifted inside of me. I was running out of patience, out of time, out of energy. And, frankly, I was tired of being polite.

How many times had we tried to work with them, only to be ignored? How many chances did we give them to be in dialogue with us only for them to dominate the conversation and refuse to be accountable? How many goddamn times could I cross my fingers in hopes that one day the US would suddenly care that the UN had called out intersex surgeries as human rights violations?

They didn't care. Nothing was changing. And I knew nothing would ever change until we forced their hand.

So I did the only thing I knew. I called up some intersex friends, and we took the fight to the streets.

CHAPTER 13

High Priority Message

Protest planned outside Lurie Children's, Thursday, Oct. 26, 2017.

Thursday, October 26, is Intersex Awareness Day and there is a planned protest outside our hospital on Chicago Avenue at noon. The protesters advocate an extreme position on the issues related to intersex individuals (who are born with signs of being both male and female). They are targeting children's hospitals nationally. Although some of the posters may be inflammatory, please be respectful.

CPD and Northwestern PD are on alert to provide support if we need it. We will have additional security staff making sure protesters do not enter the hospital and disturb families. The concierge is prepared to respond to questions from families.

Lurie Children's is one of the national leaders in this field and is a strong advocate for intersex individuals. Our Sex Development Clinic is one of a handful in the country that cares for intersex infants, children and adolescents.

If you have any questions, please contact Public Affairs at 312-227-4600.

In the years that followed my meeting with Earl, I began to slowly reshape my life's path. I knew I would need support—from my friends, my mentors, and my colleagues. I left my job at the nonprofit, Inter/Act, and began a new project with Lynnell and my friend Saifa—a Black trans intersex man, born in the Bronx, who was also in the BuzzFeed video and who, like me, had been previously diagnosed with androgen insensitivity syndrome. Lynnell, Saifa, and I came together on a phone call and laid the groundwork for what would eventually become known as the Intersex Justice Project, or IJP.

Our mission? To end invasive and unnecessary surgeries on intersex kids by taking our fight back to the streets, while empowering intersex people of color as change-makers. We were a small group, just three people, united by a common, very personal goal. Lynnell and I had stayed in touch ever since we first met at the pizza parlor. She was on the board of the Androgen Insensitivity Syndrome Differences of Sex Development (AIS-DSD) support group, where she was working hard to make the group and its annual conference more inclusive. She was also on the board at AIC, where she met Saifa, who was AIC's board's copresident.

When we met, back when I was still working for AIC, Saifa was living in Atlanta and was refreshingly not like most other people in the intersex community, let alone the world. He seemed to always be dressed in what I considered his trademark outfit: T-shirt, jeans, and comfortable—not hip—sneakers. His hair, at that time, was no fuss and shaved close. He didn't seem caught up in material things and pop-culture trends. He very much appeared to march to the beat of his own drummer.

And he's hilarious. Saifa says the wildest things, like calling almost every person in his many stories a critter, as in "and then this critter walked in the meeting talking about . . ."

Both he and Lynnell seemed to have an air of confidence about them, one that I admired greatly. They never seemed to change up who they were depending on who they were around. What you saw was what you got. They were always themselves, through and through.

Throughout the years, we would all cross paths, and sometimes we'd vent about what was going on in the intersex community, but usually we'd just dream aloud with each other or laugh at whatever hilarious story one of us, usually Saifa, was telling. In each other we found a soft place to land, one that felt a bit more sheltered and tucked away from the larger intersex community. We all seemed to easily find in one another the kind of refuge I had found early on with Lynnell.

Our comfort and ease with each other, our similar desires to shake things up and make life better for intersex people, laid the groundwork for our new organization—IJP.

We didn't have a formal status, no 501(c)(3), no funders, no office space where we could meet—none of that. Instead, we had a name, a mission, and eventually even a website! But above all else, we had what Coach Thompson would have called heart. We weren't weighed down by the conventional way of doing things.

Though other organizations with grants and funding could, theoretically, do more, they were also restricted by that same funding in the form of needing to constantly file time-sucking grant reports and other tasks. Those organizations had to be careful about what they said and how they said it because they had to be answerable to funders—and ultimately the IRS—but we weren't bogged down by those same concerns. At AIC, I had witnessed staff hem and haw for years over whether we'd stop using the language *Difference/Disorder of Sex Development (DSD)*—which many in the intersex community eschewed—in lieu of the word *intersex*. Change is often painstakingly slow in traditional organizations, such as nonprofits. IJP, on the other hand, couldn't care less about appeasing doctors by using anything other than the words *intersex* and *intersex variations* to describe our bodies.

With this nimbleness upon us, IJP swiftly decided it was time to act. But we didn't want to keep doing things the same old way. We didn't want to keep trying to play nice with doctors like Earl and his colleagues, who were seemingly digging their heels in even deeper under the guises of the *reformed* interdisciplinary clinics. We also didn't believe our success lay within the court system either, as it was slow moving, and we had recently witnessed the dismissal of the federal #Justice4MC case, with the court deciding that the surgeons responsible for harming MC couldn't be held liable because they didn't *clearly* know they were violating MC's human rights. And while the other part of the case, the lawsuit against the Medical University of South Carolina, ultimately settled out of court for $440,000, it wasn't the win we had hoped for. We needed something quicker, rougher, and dirtier.

With this, we got to work organizing a protest. It would be the first intersex protest in the US, that we knew of, since 1996, when the Intersex Society of North America had co-organized one with Transexual Menace in Boston at the American Academy of Pediatrics. Ours was planned for the same day as the first iconic protest—October 26—to happen in tandem with Intersex Awareness Day.

When my alarm clock went off that morning at 6:30 a.m., I was already awake. My body was tense and ribboned with fears I couldn't shake: the thought of the police beating us up and arresting us for protesting. Since college, I had been part of countless protests for other causes but never for intersex people. I had witnessed police at these protests break people's bones by intentionally running them over with their horses, shoot people with rubber bullets and throw flash grenades at them, and beat people with nightsticks, among other brutal acts. I couldn't shake the belief that other people wouldn't care enough about what intersex people were going through to actually take to the streets for us. I thought that no one cared about us, because hardly anyone even really knew about us.

Looking back, I think I chose to focus my energy on helping other people's causes in lieu of my own because I was afraid of doing what I knew ultimately needed to be done. I was afraid no one would show up, and I was afraid that if they did, the police might shut us down. And if people did show up, and if the police left us alone, my deepest fear was that it wouldn't work. That Lurie would just laugh at us, and our protest would be in vain. Now the day was here, and it felt so vulnerable to be heading out to fight for something so personal. I tried my best not to entertain the anxious thoughts anymore. Instead, I tried to focus on the list of things that still needed to be done.

I hit the snooze button and drifted back into a fitful sleep. I'd only gotten a couple of hours that night, and there was no way I was going to be able to get out of bed in under five snoozes. Possibly ten.

Organizing the protest had fried my nerves. It drained me of any reserves I still had. It had taken months to get the permits, to round up the people. To make signs. To make flyers. To secure bullhorns and create banners. To write speeches and promote the event on social media. While there were benefits to being a small and agile group, there were also drawbacks, one being that there were way fewer people to assign responsibilities to. Being able to organize large, complicated projects and break down all the tasks into smaller chunks with deadlines was a skill I sorely lacked. Instead, when faced with a large project, my brain became completely scattered and overwhelmed. I am a perfectionist who often procrastinates until the last minute when it comes to getting the most important things done. The result? Bone-crushing anxiety and stress that would wake me up in the middle of the night, multiple times, for weeks.

Or maybe my subconscious was trying to sabotage the protest to prevent me from going through the humiliation of choking and disappointing my entire community.

While I was lying there trying to fight through my inability to get up, a memory came to me. I was back on the softball field. Thirteen years old. And Coach Thompson was sitting beside me on the dugout bench.

I'm proud of you, Pagonis, he said in his tired smoker's voice. *It was really hot out there this weekend, and you never gave up. You went out there and you punched them in the nose like I told you to!*

"Punched them in the nose" was his way of saying I'd helped our team score a bunch of runs early on in the game.

As I lay there in bed, I realized I wasn't about to give up. It was time to get up and punch Lurie in the nose.

And suddenly I was standing. On my feet. Summoning the strength I needed to make this day happen.

My bones ached. My muscles felt dried up, like rolls of wrinkled salami. A wave of anxiety, or perhaps adrenaline, gushed through my body. I opened the Notes app on my phone and looked at my list of things to do.

1. Wake up early!
2. Go to FedEx Office and make copies.
3. Get a bullhorn.
4. Finish speech.
5. Check the RSVP list on Facebook.

I threw on some clothes, jumped in a Lyft, and rushed down to the FedEx Office one neighborhood east in the South Loop. I needed to make photocopies of our chants and the informational one-pager with our call to action, which we planned to hand out to passersby. When the clerk finally finished and handed me the crisp, warm stack of copies, I was reminded of the day I first printed out my medical records. I realized how far I'd come from that moment. Back then I was so ashamed, so unable to imagine myself telling anyone what I had read in those documents, let alone doing something as public as what I was about to do that day. In about an hour, I was going to be sharing my story over a megaphone in front of Lurie and handing out these pages to people walking by, demanding they put a stop to the nonsense and end the surgeries.

I stuffed the copies into my bag and flung myself back into the same Lyft that was idling outside. The closer we got to downtown, the more anxious I became. I began to feel carsick. I hadn't eaten that morning. I felt like if I ate, it wasn't going to stay in my stomach for long. So I went with the lesser of two bad options: not eating. And now my stomach was rumbling. I contemplated telling the driver to pull over so I could get out and puke all over Michigan Avenue.

As we drove, we crossed over the Canal Street railroad bridge, and to the left was one of my favorite views: empty train tracks that lead the eye to almost the entire Sears Tower in all of its glory. Once we crossed over into the Loop, under the "L" tracks, we were in the heart of downtown on Michigan Avenue, below all of the steel-and-glass towers. The streets were crowded with busy businesspeople in their suits and tourists with selfie sticks and American Girl doll shopping bags.

And then, in the distance, I saw it: the twenty-three-story steel-and-glass structure that was the new home of Lurie Children's Hospital. Years before, Lurie had moved from its former campus in Lincoln Park, where I was a patient, to this new downtown location.

As we got closer, I could hear my heart beating, as if I were wearing a stethoscope. I saw the sign towering over the city.

Ann & Robert H. Lurie
Children's Hospital of Chicago

Stuck in traffic, I told my driver to let me out a few blocks early, and I bolted from the Lyft. Up the street. Through the traffic. I was only about five minutes behind schedule. Or maybe ten. Probably closer to fifteen. I frantically ran for blocks through downtown Chicago until I began to hear a gurgling brook of voices. I kept running until I saw them. Saifa and Lynnell were there among a group of people, only ten to fifteen. But they were the sweetest sight I'd ever seen. They came. And more were on their way. Many of these people had promised me they would show up for me, and they did. Friends I'd known for years showed up. Some I had met in college—like Flowers and their new partner and one of their kids—and others I had met right after college who had become some of my closest friends. Friends from whom I had learned a lot about organizing and protesting. And others were people I had only recently met. Still others were complete strangers. They all had their signs out. They were unrolling the banner we had made the prior day and had their posters in hand. And in that moment, we—now a group of about twenty-five to thirty—were a family, huddled and about to protest outside the institution responsible for the anguish I had felt in my bones every single day since learning the truth. As I walked up to join this mighty group, I didn't feel as alone as I usually did in my city.

It's actually happening, I thought, and I smiled. *People actually showed up. It's game time. Let's punch 'em in the nose.*

The energy was electric. The crowd's positivity and fearlessness were contagious. I'd seen positive change due to my advocacy work before, but my work up to this point had been either giving talks or mobilizing largely online—having people sign digital petitions, sharing videos and articles, that kind of thing. This was the first in-person event of this scale that I had helped organize. Today would be the first time I'd speak directly to the hospital that had harmed me and so many others like me.

My friend Steph from IJP was the first to see me. Steph—with her fauxhawk and aviators, her cherry-red lipstick and leather jacket—ran up to me and gave me a big hug. Then she handed me a bullhorn. It felt heavy in my hand. I liked it.

"How you feeling?" she asked.

"Okay, now that I'm finally here," I replied.

Steph was a seasoned protester.

"Any updates about the police?"

"There's a few bike cops over there." She motioned with her jaw toward the alley on the side of the hospital. "They haven't come up to us yet or anything."

Bike cops. They seemed to have an inferiority complex, more so than other cops assigned to protests. I've lost track of how many times I've seen them use their bikes to beat the crap out of protesters. As I made eye contact with one of the cops, they slowly rode up to me.

"So you're the infamous Pidgeon I keep hearing about?"

"Depends on who's asking," I replied.

"Well, I just wanted to introduce myself, and let you know that we'll be here to make sure everything runs smoothly and make sure everyone stays safe," he said.

He motioned his helmeted head toward the other boys in blue standing beside their bikes near the alley.

"Thanks," I said. I felt uneasy and like I couldn't quite trust his words. I knew he and his friends were only there because Lurie had called them. Lurie had home-field advantage.

When the cop retreated to his post, I let out a big sigh of relief and rolled my eyes at him to Steph.

"You good?" Steph asked.

"Yeah, I'm great. I thought he was gonna try to shut us down. I'm so glad he didn't."

Then I saw my friend Aubree, who was making a short intersex documentary, told through the lens of my story, called *A Normal Girl*. She was there with the film's producer, Shawna; both had flown into town to document the protest for the film. Shawna waved me down to get me mic'd up.

Then I saw Saifa and walked over to give him a big hug.

"Pidgeon!" he yelled into my ear as he squeezed me tight. "You finally made it, homie!"

Saifa was always quick to let me know when I was late.

"I'm sorry I'm late," I said. "How you doing? Everything good?"

"Oh, I'm great!" he said, drawing out the *r*'s like Tony the Tiger. "There are so many fine-ass people here!"

The whites of his eyes grew wide, and he looked around at people in the crowd forming beside us.

"Oh my God, Saifa," I said, smiling, rolling my eyes yet again.

"Homie, I love Chicago!"

By which he meant those in Chicago who identified as femme.

"And Chicago loves you."

"Did you get the copies?" Saifa asked.

"Here they are," I said. I handed him two stacks of paper. He then looked me in the eye.

"You ready, homie?"

I nodded. Adrenaline was flooding through my body. I looked down at the flyer and focused on the words I'd written in fancy cursive: *Intersex Is Beautiful.*

"Let's get it cracking, homie!" Saifa said. Then he put a bullhorn to his lips.

"How's everyone doing?" he shouted. His words blared out of the tinny speakers.

The crowd roared.

"I said, 'How's everyone doing?'" he asked again, louder this time.

The crowd cheered even louder, and the chants began to echo off Lurie's glass facade.

Autonomy, not surgery!
Keep your scalpels off of me!

To the right of the banner, I saw Flowers, their partner, Ash, and their child, Nova. Nova was only five or six and wearing a knitted blue monster hat with adorable yellow horns and googly eyes sewn on top. They were the youngest person I knew who identified as nonbinary. They were born with a neurological condition called hydrocephalus, and because of it, they'd spent a lot of time as a patient at Lurie. As a result, Nova literally became one of their poster children after they used Nova's image and story in one of their ad campaigns. And now they were here with two of their parents, bravely standing in solidarity. The three of them were a sight to behold.

Ash was crouched beside Nova, eye level with them, and they were holding a small rectangular yellow protest sign in their hands that read Fix Your Hearts, Not Our Parts.

My heart was tickled when I looked around and took in the scene. Years of hard work all culminating in that moment, marked by people chanting and thrusting their hand-painted signs in the air.

Surgery is not the solution,
it's the problem

No justice, no peace!
No intersex surgery!

187

In the middle of everyone was a giant banner painted with big black block letters that read:

Stop harming intersex children!
#LurieEndSurgery

To the right of those words was a big blue child's hand, just like the one used in Lurie's logo, except ours had red paint dripping from it to symbolize the blood they drew from intersex kids when they performed unnecessary surgeries on us.

Everyone entering the hospital that sunny fall afternoon, or curiously peering through the floor-to-ceiling windows that made up the front of Lurie's imposing skyscraper facade, was confronted with our message. They could no longer look away. We were here, and we would keep coming back until they stopped these barbaric practices on intersex kids.

As our protest made its way closer to Lurie's front doors, people who were present took turns speaking into the bullhorn. One of those people was IJP's cofounder, and my first intersex friend, Lynnell, who talked about her story and why the surgeries needed to end. Then it was my turn. I put Steph's megaphone to my lips. With shallow breath, a racing heart, and hands that were shaking as if I had just seen a ghost, I winged it.

"This hospital knows that intersex people exist," I said, my words echoing into the sky. "But they refuse to believe we can be left alone in the bodies we were born with. And that's why we're here demanding bodily integrity—not just for intersex people but for all people!"

The drumming of my heart began to drown out the sounds of everything else around me. I was going to pass out. The thrill was exhilarating.

Then I remembered the internal memo that Lurie had sent to all of its employees, alerting them of our protest. The one that said we had an extreme position.

"We do have an extreme position! And it's simply this: we just want people to be able to grow up in the bodies they were born with and be able to make decisions on their own when they're older."

The crowd erupted.

When I was done speaking, my shoulders relaxed, and my eyes narrowed as I rejoined the crowd and handed the megaphone back to Saifa. I felt myself taking a bit of breath. I was worried the cops would shut our permitless protest down or make unnecessary arrests. But they just sat by and let us do our thing. Electric jolts coursed through my veins, and I realized in that moment that I felt both proud and powerful.

I hoped what I'd said made sense and resonated with the folks who could hear it. I also desperately hoped the sound of my message was able to permeate Lurie's twenty-three stories of glass so those with their noses scrunched up against the windows, nervously peering down upon us, could also hear me.

⚮

Near the end of our demonstration, one of our volunteers handed a flyer to a woman in blue scrubs who was just off her hospital shift. I paid careful attention. As Saifa pumped people up with another megaphone chant, I watched this woman furrow her brow as she processed what she was reading. I began to make my way closer. Now I was within earshot of her when she asked, "Wait, this still goes on?"

"Yes, it does," I said. "It happened to me when I was a kid. And it's still happening to many others today."

"But here?" she said, motioning with her head toward the hospital. "At Lurie? They're still doing this here?" She couldn't quite take it all in. She looked to be in a state of dismay. Or maybe it was shock.

"Yes," I said.

She exhaled in a tone that punctuated her exasperation and surprise.

"That's why we're here today," I said. "We're demanding that your hospital become the first to end these cruel and unnecessary surgeries on intersex kids. We want Lurie to become the first in the nation to do the right thing, to be an example for the other hospitals doing the same thing."

"I can't believe this," she said, shaking her head and scanning the scene beside us.

"Thank you for coming out to speak to us and to learn about what's going on at your job," I said. "We need all the support we can get."

"Would you like to sign up for our mailing list to stay informed?" the person next to me with a clipboard asked.

"Of course!" she said. "I am pissed! I'll be writing an email to my boss first thing in the morning and telling them how upset I am!"

At that moment, my friend Aubree, who was able to hear the conversation via a tiny wireless microphone that was taped underneath my T-shirt, walked up to us with her hefty video camera in tow.

"Would you be willing to go on camera to have a conversation with us?"

"Yes, I would!"

I was shocked she had agreed. I figured there was no way an employee would be brave enough to stand up to Lurie on the record.

Right then, her phone grabbed her attention, and she whipped it out of her bag.

"Oh no! I'm late! Take my number and I'll do the interview later. I promise!"

I couldn't believe someone from the inside actually cared.

It may have been just one person, with hundreds, if not thousands, still to go, but at least we had one ally on the inside. And having one person made me realize that getting through to some of the people on the inside was possible. It made me realize that what we were doing that day mattered. It also made me realize that there were probably so many other employees just like her who didn't even know what was going on right underneath their noses.

Our work was just beginning.

CHAPTER 14

The next year, on Intersex Awareness Day in 2018, we organized a different kind of demonstration: a train takeover. By this time, Lynnell had taken a step back from IJP, leaving just Saifa and me in charge. We led dozens of our Chicago supporters onto different Chicago Transit Authority (CTA) train cars. Once we were all in a car together, with loud voices (apologies to the ears of the people who were on the train that day!), we'd read in unison from a printed script we had prepared. We alerted passengers, many of whom were Chicagoans and familiar with Lurie's reputation—thanks to its near-constant barrage of advertising on billboards, buses, trains, and bus stops—about a different side of the city's beloved hospital. We shouted over the grinding sounds of the train's wheels to let passengers know about what Dr. Earl Cheng and his group of colleagues were doing to their intersex patients. After all, as Coach Thompson always said, there is no I in team.

After we finished our script, we invited willing train-goers to take a photo holding up a dry-erase board we brought along with us that read Dear Lurie: Make Chicago proud and be the first hospital to #EndIntersexSurgery.

Before exiting to get on a different train car, we hung posters, each with a different intersex fact on the bottom. And on top was our call to action:

No One Deserves a Forced Sex Change
and This Is Especially True for Vulnerable Children

Lurie Children's Hospital: Make Chicago Proud!
Become the First Hospital in the US to Ban Intersex
Genital Surgery

There was no stopping us from spreading our message, not just at Lurie but to everyone in the city. We hoped that spreading the word across the city would increase pressure on Lurie to do the right thing.

The winter after our train takeover, I got word that the American Urological Association's annual meeting was taking place on May 3, 2019, in Chicago at McCormick Place, the largest convention center in all of North America. Earl would be there, representing his post in an AUA subgroup, the Society of Pediatric Urology, which meant IJP would be there.

After scouting the area in advance, we decided to settle on a spot just off to the side of the convention center's front doors, across from the entrance to a hotel. We chose that spot because it wasn't blocking the flow of any sidewalk foot traffic, making the likelihood of arrest during our unpermitted protest less likely, we believed. We also picked that spot because it was visible to the conference attendees coming and going all day.

It was early when folks started to arrive. As the spot began to fill up, I scanned the crowd for faces I could recognize. Saifa was there, and so were Flowers and their partner, Ash, along with their older child, Nova, and their newest child, Sól—still an infant. Sarah-Ji, my closest friend, was off to the side busily documenting the day with her trusty Nikon. My roommate Gaby; my friends Monica, Debbie, Shaka, Ric, and Theo; and my neighbors Grae and Jennie were all there. Carrie—a friend and a disability rights activist I had met while doing *The Vagina Monologues* in college—was there in her motorized wheelchair. Steph was in attendance, trusty bullhorn in hand. There were also people I didn't know, like an intersex person and their partner who had heard about the event on social media and driven a couple of hours up from southern Illinois. They were decked out, like most of us, in the intersex flag's colors of purple and yellow, and had matching poms-poms to boot. There was even an intersex person who had been in the audience at one of IJP's events the previous year—and they let us know it was their first time being out as intersex. As I scanned the faces, I froze. Like a pixelated mirage slowly coming into focus, a familiar face materialized—it was one that I never thought I'd see at any protest, much less an intersex protest.

It was my mother.

It was brisk out but sunny, and she had on a light-black winter jacket, blue jeans, and black sheepskin boots. There was a piece of folded-up notebook paper clutched in her hand.

I made my way toward her, shocked. "You came?"

She nodded and wiped a tear from her cheek. We had only just recently reconnected and were attempting to repair our relationship. I had texted her about the protest, but I wasn't sure if she'd show up.

I hugged her.

"Thanks for coming, Mom," I said.

"Of course," she said. "I like your face paint. It reminds me of when you played softball and would put the black streaks under your eyes."

"Want some?" I asked her.

"Sure, why not?" She smiled.

I smudged purple-and-yellow stripes of face paint across each of her cheekbones, just like I had done to myself and a few of the other attendees.

Then a nonbinary friend named Jess walked up to us and asked my mom if she would like a sign. My mom took one from the pile in Jess's hands. She then took a place among the others in the crowd who were beginning to assemble. They were holding up the new yellow-and-purple banner we had painted earlier in the week; it featured IJP's logo—a purple rose because roses are known in botany as "perfect" flowers, since they are "hermaphroditic"—and the words *End Intersex Surgery* in big black letters. There among the group, across the street from the entrance to the conference, where attendees were starting to peer at us through the windows, was my mom, proudly holding up a sign that read:

LURIE CHILDREN'S
WHAT THE HELL?
KIDS SHOULD CHOOSE
FOR THEMSELVES!

Seeing her there, boldly painted and holding up her sign, was one of those things in life I didn't know how badly I needed until after it happened. Her presence in the action that afternoon in front of all those surgeons and doctors—the likes of whom led her and my father astray when I was a kid—helped me understand that she was not only sorry for allowing them to hurt me like they did but also proud of me. All of me. Even the hurt and intersex parts of me. And she wasn't ashamed to let Lurie, and anyone else who happened to walk by that afternoon, know. We'd come such a long way from that first conversation at the kitchen table.

She knew she couldn't change the past. But she could walk along-side me in the future. At one point, when we asked if anyone in the crowd wanted to take a turn saying anything, my mom stepped for-ward. She took out that piece of folded paper with some notes she had prepared, by hand, and Saifa held the megaphone close to her mouth. She spoke from her heart. She told everyone in attendance that what had happened to her, and her kid, at the hands of Lurie shouldn't hap-pen to anyone else. She let Lurie, and all the pediatric urologists from different cities, know that what they were doing to intersex kids needed to stop. She let anyone within earshot know, and those watching at home on the live stream, that as a parent of a former intersex patient, she knew that what they're doing to intersex kids is wrong. That day, my mother showed up to support her intersex baby.

❦

The two years after IJP's first protest in 2017 were a whirlwind of other protests, poster making and sharing, Twitter power hours, collaborations, workshops, panels, and other activities and actions meant to further our #EndIntersexSurgery campaign. During that time, Saifa and I had opened to the idea of also incorporating a legal strategy into our campaign after we were put in touch with the ACLU. We attended many phone and in-person meetings with a pair of ACLU lawyers in the hopes that they would be able to help us in our campaign against Lurie and possibly even launch a lawsuit. But after a year and a half of bureaucratic red tape, we had only gotten as far as sending Lurie a stern letter on ACLU letterhead.

The letter plainly said that Lurie was in violation of two Illinois state laws by allowing the surgeries to continue—one for informed consent and another that prohibited female genital mutilation. We had hoped that if Lurie knew it was possibly in violation of two preexisting state laws, maybe it'd call off the surgeries.

When we finally got a response from Lurie, it was in the form of an emailed letter. The email, a few short paragraphs typed on Lurie's letterhead, could basically be summed up by the following two sentences:

Thanks, but no thanks.

Sincerely, Lurie Legal.

❦

As usual, Lurie continued to show us that it couldn't care less about our campaign.

Despite all the protests, meetings, and actions, after 2019, the years seemed to begin slipping by without much movement. I worked for myself as an intersex speaker with a few other side hustles to help pay the bills, like a nonbinary clothing line I launched called Too Cute to Be Binary. I moved from Rogers Park to Pilsen. I taught two classes at DePaul—Social Media for Social Justice and Intro to LGBTQ+ Studies. A few years later, I bought my first house. A place just for me. After nearly a decade of giving intersex talks around the world and having a few side hustles, I was able to save up enough money to be able to afford a down payment on a home. When I first saw the handsome graystone, built in 1903, I fell in love. It was on a sunny corner next to an empty lot on the west side of the city. Fifteen minutes from where I grew up when we lived with Gram and Gramps in the building on Austin Avenue. A statuesque graystone on a street lined with enormous oak trees. Within moments of stepping inside for the first time, I turned to my Realtor and said, "This is the one."

I had finally found my home.

Despite the joy of a new home, I could feel the exhaustion of all the fighting with Lurie setting in. I could feel I was burning out.

In my post with IJP, I had helped to raise tons of awareness and to build a coalition who supported our campaign, but I had yet to meet a single Lurie employee who would publicly speak out against them and cosign our campaign. The Lurie workers we had met at prior protests had all declined to speak publicly.

But that all changed when I crossed paths with a supernova.

Supernovas are the largest explosions to ever have been recorded in space. At their peak brightness, supernovas can—for just a moment—outshine the entire galaxy.

I first met Ellie Kim at a Dyke March a year after IJP's first protest. I was hawking Too Cute to Be Binary merch at a vendor table when Ellie approached. She was a striking, femme, Asian American trans woman. She purchased a tote and a sticker. We chatted a bit. And then she evaporated into the crowd of people.

Moments later, my friend Sarah-Ji leaned over and, with her hand up to my ear so Ellie couldn't see, whispered, "Do you know who that was?"

"Ellie?"

"Oh my God, Pidgeon, that's SuperKnova!" she said with a huge smile.

"Who?"

"SUPERKNOVA!"

Sarah-ji was practically gasping at that point.

"What do you mean?"

"That's Ellie's stage name," Sarah-Ji said. "She plays electric guitar. Her solo project name is SuperKnova!"

The look of exasperation on Sarah-Ji's face was precious, but I had no idea what she was talking about.

As I turned around to search through my clear Rubbermaid bins of merchandise, Ellie's stage name lingered in my mind. SuperKnova!

"Damn, that's a beautiful name."

❀☙✂☙❀

The second time I crossed paths with SuperKnova, it was no accident. It was summer in Chicago, and I was lost somewhere between the felt-green pool table and the old-school photo booth in a Ukrainian Village venue. Sarah-Ji had invited me to the show. The walls of the Empty Bottle were a chaos of band stickers, rock-show flyers, and layers of etchings that had been carved into the plaster over the years. The thick waft of cheap beer emanated from the floor and flooded my nostrils.

After playing a round of pool, Sarah-Ji and I made our way toward the stage. I ordered a drink at the bar and stared, mesmerized by the haphazardly strung, twinkly Christmas lights pinned behind the bar.

It was my first time seeing Ellie perform as SuperKnova. It was also probably my first time ever seeing anyone perform solo with an electric guitar. I wasn't prepared for what came next.

Supernovas occur in space when giant stars, exponentially larger than our sun, explode into a spectacular paroxysm of colored gas, light, and dust.

SuperKnova got up on that stage rocking a miniskirt and long black hair. Suddenly, bone-chilling riffs were interspersed with exquisitely plucked notes blasted out of her hot-pink electric guitar. I was unable to look away, completely captivated by the magic that enveloped me. The contrast between her legendary Hendrixesque shredding skills and her centered stage presence was captivating. The stereotypical rock 'n' roller, Ellie was not.

She was iconic. I immediately became a fan.

After the show, I approached Ellie at the merch table that was set up just outside the club. Ellie was busy signing autographs for fans.

"Ellie?" I said. "It's me, Pidgeon. We met a while back, at a Dyke March."

"Pidgeon!" she said with a smile. "I remember."

"You were amazing up there!"

"Oh, it's just a fun thing I do on the side," she said.

"On the side?"

She nodded. "Yeah, in my other life, I'm a doctor. At Lurie."

My heart stopped. My chest tightened. It was as if the universe had placed this human being in my life. I had been searching, desperately, for years to find a doctor inside Lurie to be an ally.

"Listen," I said, "I don't want to overstep, but I was a patient there . . . when I was a kid. Do you think we could talk sometime?"

Ellie nodded. A seriousness came over her, adjusting her demeanor. She seemed to sense how important the topic was for me. "Anytime."

I bought a T-shirt, and Ellie wrote her number down on the receipt.

I didn't know what would come of this chance encounter, but I had a feeling that I'd just met a person who could help me change the world.

If IJP was going to get Lurie to agree to our demands to end intersex surgeries, then we needed to ride our shock wave of momentum and build a powerful, citywide coalition. At this point, IJP was just a two-person volunteer operation: Saifa and myself. But we had started to work more with other people and organizations, such as interACT and Human Rights Watch, in order to increase our capacity.

One of the key people we teamed up with was my friend Steph, whom I had met years before when I gave a talk at her college. She was the associate executive director of an organization on the South Side called Brave Space Alliance. Her group helped serve the trans, intersex, and gender-nonconforming communities. She was also a local politics nerd.

Still, taking on an organization like Lurie, which had wealth, prestige, and countless legal resources, was a massive undertaking for such a small team. The deck was stacked against us.

Under Steph's guidance, we started reaching out to organizations we believed might be willing to work with us as allies in our new quest to pass legislation banning intersex surgery in Illinois. One of those people was Representative Kelly Cassidy.

"Who's that?" I asked Steph on the train one day.

"She's an Illinois congresswoman," she said. "And also just so happens to be a badass lesbian. And I'm her constituent!"

I smiled. Steph was the only person I knew who would ever refer to themself as a constituent.

"When I get off the train, I'm gonna stop by her office and try to get us a meeting," she said.

A few hours later, I received a text from Steph confirming that she had set up a meeting with Representative Cassidy for September. We had about four months to prepare.

The following week, I woke up with a headache that got worse as the day went on. By the afternoon, I couldn't take it anymore. I tugged my black linen curtains shut and lay back down in my bed. As I did, I made the nap-defying mistake of looking at my phone. In my DMs was an interesting message from a stranger. They asked if I had seen Lurie's Instagram page.

"They've been posting all these pictures of trans celebrities," they said. "Trying to show how much they care about trans kids. Meanwhile, they're still doing surgeries on intersex kids!"

I quickly found Lurie's account and started scrolling. As I looked at the photographs, I began to feel rage boiling up inside of me. One photo struck a nerve: a photo of a friend, Indya Moore. Indya is a non-binary Dominican-Boricua model and actor from the Bronx, and they were a star on the hit show *Pose*, a series detailing the struggles of the Black and Brown trans ballroom scene in 1980s New York. After *Pose* hit the air, they quickly rose to fame—especially in the LGBTQIA+ community. Their fame reached the covers of *Elle* and *Teen Vogue*, and their social media followers numbered in the millions. I first met them on Instagram, when Indya shared about some of the work we were doing at IJP. Six months later, we connected in Chicago when they were in town visiting their former partner. In 2019, the year we met, *TIME* named them on its list of the 100 Most Influential People in the World. I was about to discover just how influential they were.

After I found the Instagram page of Lurie's gender development clinic, I immediately FaceTimed Indya. They had their phone on a Citi Bike phone mount and were riding through the city with a helmet on.

"Hey, Pagona," they said. "What's your tea, gurl?"

"Indya! I just found out Lurie's gender clinic, the one that sees trans and intersex kids, has an Instagram page. And on it they posted all these pictures of trans celebrities. Including you!"

"Bitch, what?"

"Yes, bitch."

"Biiiiitch."

Their brows were sparring with one another.

"I know, gurl. They're using all of your images to paint a rosy picture of the trans portion of their clinic, while conveniently glossing over the intersex portion."

"Oh, hell naw. Uh-uh. Nope. Send it to me."

"Say less."

"Wait, bitch, are you naked?"

"Yes, gurl, I have a headache and was trying to sleep it off. But then I saw this!"

I really hadn't had time to get decent before I called her.

We said our goodbyes.

A few minutes later, Indya went live on their personal Instagram page. The broadcast was titled "In Solidarity with Intersex Communities."

In the live, they talked about IJP's campaign to end intersex surgeries at Lurie. They mentioned how furious they were that Lurie's page was using their image. I watched in awe.

"You wanna lift up trans people by stepping on the necks of intersex people?" they asked defiantly.

Indya explained to their millions of followers what intersexuality is and the injustices we have been forced to endure at places like Lurie.

Then, toward the end of the broadcast, they asked their viewers to join them in commenting on Lurie's page. "Tell them we demand they end intersex surgeries!"

Within minutes, Lurie's Instagram was flooded with comments from all over the world. The onslaught continued for weeks. IJP's campaign went viral. Lurie couldn't post anything new without hundreds of people commenting #EndIntersexSurgery within hours.

Lurie, for once, had lost the upper hand.

Other trans celebrities, like Angelica Ross and Hunter Schafer, responded to Indya's call for support and demanded the clinic end the unnecessary intersex surgeries on kids.

At one point, cis allies, like celebrity Gabrielle Union, joined the fight to show their support for our campaign too. And then an unexpected voice joined the onslaught.

Dr. Ellie Kim started posting on Twitter. Like a comet in the night sky, SuperKnova herself appeared and awed. She hyperlaunched the momentum of our campaign even further. Finally—*finally*—we had a voice on the inside publicly stating that they did not agree with their hospital's practices.

On July 13, 2020, as the crescent moon began to rise, I sat at the black vanity desk in my room and turned on the light bulbs that surrounded my mirror. Before reaching for my eyeliner in the drawer, my hand made a pit stop at my phone, and within seconds I was on Twitter. I found myself disoriented and lost in the Twitterverse, not quite sure why I had launched the app in the first place. The habit of checking IJP's social media pages had become second nature.

My thumb instinctively clicked on the mentions tab, and once it loaded, I saw SuperKnova's account had mentioned IJP's handle. I immediately clicked on it to read more. Her thread read:

> (1/4) I am a trans woman, physician and employee of @LurieChildrens Hospital. I categorically stand against the medically UNNECESSARY surgeries / interventions being performed on intersex kids by pediatric urologists at this institution and the complicity of my own dept Adol Med

> (2/4) The intersex community, medical organizations like the AAFP, the WHO, GLMA and Lurie's own queer and trans employees have been calling on Earl Cheng

and others to cease these harmful interventions. Every time they have been dismissed and disregarded.

(3/4) I will not stay silent on the matter until these mutilations [are] stopped. Intersex bodies are beautiful and perfect the way they are and any medical interventions should be up to the individual. NOT bigoted parents wanting a "normal" child, not hospitals, not doctors. PERIOD.

(4/4) I stand with the intersex community. Sign the petition (https://bit.ly/2DfyCF7) and support, follow, direct funds to @Pidgejen and @IntersexJustice

Never, to my knowledge, in the history of intersex activism had an employee of a children's hospital spoken out so publicly against what happened to intersex people. We had many people say they would, but ultimately, they never did. With one fierce Twitter thread, that had all changed.

As I read those tweets, I felt chills shiver up and down my spine like flashes of lightning. We had entered unchartered territory. After years of protests, and the swell of support our campaign received after Indya boosted it, I had hoped that Lurie had been losing some steam, but now, with all these new allies, IJP definitely began to feel the tide turning.

In the week that followed, four more Lurie employees followed in the footsteps of Dr. Ellie Kim and exhibited cataclysmic bravery. The dominoes were falling. These fellow employees called out their employer for its complicity in the harm of intersex kids. One of those employees, I discovered, was intersex.

Supernovas are mammoth eruptions that take place at the end of a star's life cycle. IJP wouldn't be silent any longer. We wouldn't have to fake it until we made it anymore. IJP was still a small two-person operation: Saifa and me. But our collaborations with other individuals and organizations, especially Brave Space Alliance, interACT, and Human Rights Watch, were stronger than ever. At this point, we were in regular communication to strategize around how to make the most of this moment we found ourselves in. And, suddenly, there was a new player in the fight: SuperKnova. A supernova's shock waves swell across space and time, leaving no nearby interstellar stone unturned. The universe, it seemed, was aligning.

Our meeting with Representative Kelly Cassidy took place a few months later. The morning of the meeting, I was running late yet again. I tried to find decent shoes, threw on a light jacket, and floored the gas pedal. I took a deep breath and looked out my passenger-side window at Navy Pier's Centennial Wheel. My parents had taken my sister, Nicole, and me there once when they were trying to work things out after their divorce. My dad bought tickets to the Ferris wheel that overlooked the lake and the skyscrapers. My mother stayed down below.

"I'm good right here on the ground," she snapped when we tried to get her to come on the ride.

"It's so peaceful up here, huh, guys?" my dad asked, as my sister and I took in the view.

I had never seen my dad look so at ease.

He pointed out the boats on the lake below and declared to the winds whipping around us how one day he would have a boat he could take us out on.

My family looked beautiful suspended high against the burnt-orange sky. I twisted in my seat and reached my tiny arm between the safety bars to wave to my mom. She nervously waved back with both hands.

It gave me a feeling of peace to remember a time when my family was together. Even if things weren't perfect, we were still fighting to be whole. The moment helped me escape my worried mind for a moment. I felt the anxiety retreat from my body.

When I arrived outside the office, I parked down the street, grabbed my bag, and hauled ass toward the front door. As I sprinted inside, Coach Thompson's voice barked in my mind.

HUSTLE, PAGONIS!

I took a beat to catch my breath, just barely, before opening my mouth again to speak to the person sitting behind the front desk.

"I'm here for a meeting with Representative Cassidy."

"Your name?"

"Pidgeon," I replied. "Pagonis."

They stood up and led me to the back of the office. As I followed the receptionist through the tiny maze of corridors, I was surprised at how casual the space felt. I was expecting formal, gray, and stuffy. But, instead, it was more reminiscent of the offices of nonprofits and community centers. The casualness helped me feel a bit more relaxed.

As we approached the open door of Representative Cassidy's office, laughter erupted. It sounded genuine, as if old friends were rehashing memories. I could hear Stephanie's voice. I took a deep breath, tugged on the bottom of my button-up, and stepped inside.

It was a cozy space that took me back to the offices of my women's and gender studies professors. Kelly Cassidy was seated behind a desk. One of her campaign posters was on the wall behind her. She greeted me with a warm smile and inviting eyes. My knotted-up stomach received the message that it was okay I was a few minutes late.

"Hello, everyone," I said with a shy smile.

"Pidgeon!" Steph beamed.

"Hi, Steph! Hello, everyone."

As I scanned the small office, I was caught off guard that two people I didn't expect to be joining us were there.

"Pidgeon, this is Lea Negron, my chief of staff," Kelly said. "She'll be taking notes today."

"Nice to meet you, Lea."

"The pleasure is all mine," she said.

"And this is . . . well, why don't you go ahead and introduce yourself," she said to the other woman in the room.

"My name is Khadine Bennett, and I'm the director of advocacy and intergovernmental affairs at ACLU Illinois."

Hearing her say she was from the ACLU put me on alert. IJP had already run into so many dead ends working with their organization. Years of stalled meetings and unproductive calls. When they finally drafted a letter to Lurie—in tandem with IJP—suggesting the institution had broken the law, the letter had little impact. Just hearing the acronym made me feel exhausted, but I was willing to give Khadine a chance. We hadn't worked together before, and in coalition-building work, beggars couldn't be choosy.

"I hope it's okay that Khadine joins us this afternoon," Representative Kelly chimed in. "Khadine and I have worked together in the past on getting some progressive legislation passed, and I invited her to our meeting today because I think she could possibly be a valuable partner as we move forward."

"Yes, that's right," Khadine said. "And I've also heard that you've been working with some of my colleagues at ACLU for a while, and I wanted to see if there's anything I could possibly do to help."

"Yes, of course," I said. "I'm so glad you're joining us! IJP has been working with the ACLU for a couple of years now. It's so wonderful to meet you!"

I pulled up a chair and took a seat beside Stephanie. When I finally settled in, Stephanie and I began to share our hopes with Kelly's team. IJP's goal was ambitious: to write and pass a bill in Illinois that made it illegal for doctors to perform surgeries on intersex kids.

"I'm in!" Kelly said.

Lea's fingers were busy typing away notes as Kelly looked at Khadine, who nodded in agreement.

"I think it's a great idea," Khadine said. "I would love to help out in any way I can."

I wasn't accustomed to people knowing, let alone caring, about intersex people, and now I had an elected official and an ACLU lawyer in my presence who didn't even bat a lash when we proposed a bill to end intersex surgeries. I had to take a moment to process things.

"Before we move forward on the bill, though," Kelly said, "I think it might be a good idea for me to bring this idea to the LGBTQ+ caucus and strategize with my colleagues."

I wasn't familiar with the caucus, but I was down for any help we could get. I nodded as she went on. "I'll gauge their interest, which I expect to be high, and see if they have the capacity to work on this with us. I think we can start with something like a letter from our caucus. Since I also sit on the appropriations committee, they might be inclined to pay attention."

That's when I sat up even higher, imagining the faces of Lurie's lawyers when they got this new letter freshly typed on Illinois House of Representatives letterhead. It was a glorious thought.

After Representative Cassidy met with her colleagues in the LGBTQ+ caucus in the Illinois House, they quickly agreed to jointly investigate what was going on at Lurie. Pretty soon, a meeting was on the books.

Kelly later recounted the story of their meeting. It took place on a cold February morning. Kelly and her colleagues in the LGBTQ+ caucus trekked downtown for the 10:00 a.m. meeting at Lurie. Once there, Lurie's chief external affairs officer and senior vice president, Susan Hayes Gordon, led them to the room where the meeting was scheduled.

Inside the meeting room, they were greeted by Lurie's chief medical officer, Dr. Derek Wheeler; the associate director of community programs and initiatives, Jennifer Leininger (yes, the same Jennifer Leininger from the basement meeting years prior); and the division head of pediatric urology, Dr. Earl Cheng, whom I'd already met in that first meeting after my interview aired on WBEZ.

The agenda said the official purpose of the meeting was to discuss Lurie Children's policies on surgery for intersex children.

"We are fully aware of all of the good that occurs here at Lurie," Kelly said. "Which is why, and my apologies if it seems like we're repeating ourselves, we're so confused by your harmful policies and actions when it comes to your intersex patients. Why treat them different?"

Earl spoke up in his own defense.

"I can't tell you how many parents of intersex babies have thanked me for fixing their babies' defects," he said. "'Now my baby can have a normal life, thanks to you, Dr. Cheng, and your amazing clinic,' they tell me all the time."

"What type of defects are they referring to?"

"Some girls are born with clitoral birth defects," Earl replied. "And if these activists get their way, if we couldn't do corrective surgeries anymore, it would be unfair to those parents and their little girls, for whom surgery is really the only option."

When the meeting was over, Lurie's employees thanked Representative Cassidy and her colleagues for bringing our concerns to their attention.

"We will follow up," said Susan Hayes Gordon, reaching out to shake hands with everyone as they filed out.

And then, almost a half year later, what seemed like the impossible happened. Shortly before noon, on July 28—just two weeks after Indya and Ellie garnered millions of views on social media—I received a phone call from a number I didn't recognize. It was Representative Kelly Cassidy.

"Pidgeon?"

"Yes?"

"Pidgeon, are you there? It's Kelly Cassidy."

There was an urgency in her voice laced with something else I couldn't quite place.

"Yes, I'm here."

"Pidgeon, we did it!" Her voice was trembling.

"We did it?" I genuinely did not know what she meant.

"It's over, Pidgeon. It's over. They're ending the surgeries."

She was in tears.

"What? Are you sure? How do you know?"

I wasn't able to believe the words coming out of her mouth. Tears welled up in my eyes. My center of gravity suddenly felt shaky. My vision blurred.

"Lurie just sent me an email. I just forwarded it to you and Saifa. They said they're stopping. It's over, Pidgeon. We did it. We fucking did it!"

Hearing her get so emotional opened my own floodgates, and the tears started rolling out.

"Oh my God, I can't believe this, I can't believe this, I can't believe this," I repeated.

When I hung up the phone, I started sobbing.

When I was able to gather myself up a bit, I called Indya on FaceTime. They were in the shower when I told them the news. Steam surrounded them. My face instantly started contorting into all types of ugly, and the tears, like tails of comets and shards of icy asteroids, began gushing, sliding down my cheeks.

When I was finally able to get the words out, all I could say was thank you.

"For what?"

"Thank you for helping us," I squeezed out.

"With what, Pidgeon?"

"They're ending the surgeries. Lurie. They apologized. They're not going to do it anymore. We did it, Indya. We did it!"

I called Saifa next. After we hung up, I spent the rest of the day on the phone with everyone near and dear to the campaign, telling them the news. I was radiantly buzzing on a cosmic cloud.

We did it.

EPILOGUE

A few months after moving into my new house, I took three of my young cousins—Jordan, Bre, and Bella—to a poultry feedstore on the northwest side of the city, close to where I grew up, and let them each pick out a baby chick to grow up and live in my new backyard.

"Are they boys or girls?" my cousin Jordan asked the hefty Balkan man seated behind the cash register. He and his wife were the feedstore's longtime owners.

"All chickens are girls," he said. "Like all yous. Boy chickens are called roosters. None of our chicks for sale are roosters. No one wants them."

"Pidgeon is a they," Bella said.

He looked confused.

"Pigeons are different," he said. "Wait, do you guys want pigeons or chickens?"

"We're here for chickens," I chimed in. I had a smile I couldn't hold back.

"Wait, how will they lay eggs if there are no roosters?" Bre asked. She was genuinely stumped.

Sensing her cue, the Balkan man's wife responded, "Chickens don't need roosters to lay eggs. Their eggs are like a period for them. You know how women like your mommy have periods? Well, chickens have periods every day, and that's how the eggs come out."

Everyone, including me, was quiet for a moment as we chewed on this revelatory information. And like a baby chick cracking through its shell, Bella broke the silence.

"Pidgeon isn't our mom," she corrected the Balkan man's wife.

"Yeah, that's our cousin." Jordan giggled.

I was honored to be mistaken for their parent because I love them so much. When people make that assumption, it makes my heart do a backflip.

With both hands on Bella's shoulders now, I smiled awkwardly at the store owners. I took a deep breath, letting the wafting aroma of anise in the shop fill my chest. "Okay," I said, exhaling, "thanks for teaching us *all* that."

Then I turned to my cousins. "Now why don't you each pick out a baby chick and we'll take them home."

⚶

As I pulled into my driveway, some of my neighbors saw us pulling up. Quida, a slender woman with eyes like sunlit jasper, saw the box I was carrying and hollered from her porch.

"Hey, Pidgeon! What you got in that box?"

"Baby chicks!"

Quida was the second neighbor I met and got to know on my new block. She was out on her back porch the day I was moving in. Her child, Amira, and her niece, Kamoorah, were seven and eight. They heard the commotion and became excited. Their round brown eyes lit up like fireworks as they hurried over to me.

"I missed you," Amira squealed.

"Me too!" Kamoorah added as they both hugged a different side of my waist.

Quida walked over toward the alley where we stood. As she approached me, she said, "Pidgeon, do you want to have kids? 'Cuz you can have these two since they're so obsessed with you."

"I can't have children," I said.

"Can I see the chickens?" Amira asked.

"Me too?" Kamoorah pleaded.

"Of course."

Amira's hair was parted down the middle and sectioned into six equal braided parts. She was wearing a snow cone–blue sweater with an image of a princess on it. Her toenails were painted with the remnants of neon-pink nail polish. Kamoorah, in a neon-salmon tennis skirt, had waist-length box braids.

Out of nowhere, Kamoorah then made some noises, sounding something out. "Soo-per-kay-no . . . HUH?"

"Girl, what you sayin'?" Quida snapped.

"I'm trying to read what's on Pidgeon's shirt. What's your shirt say, Pidgeon?" Kamoorah asked.

I looked down and saw I was wearing the SuperKnova T-shirt that I had bought at Ellie's performance.

"Oooh, it says SuperKnova! It's the name of my friend's music project. She plays electric guitar."

"Ohhhhhh," Kamoorah said.

"What's a superknova?" Amira asked.

"A supernova is what happens when stars in outer space die. Their explosive deaths are crazy beautiful, and guess what I just found out?" I gushed.

"What?"

"The universe is so big that when we see a supernova here on earth, they aren't happening in that moment. They actually happened millions, sometimes billions, of years ago!"

As I continued to explain all the things I found interesting about supernovas, I smiled to myself with a newfound appreciation for the journey a supernova must go on before it gets seen. I could relate. The work IJP and our allies did with Lurie started years ago. And the broader intersex rights movement started decades prior to that. And for centuries before that, there have always been intersex people. Silently existing, scared and forced to live in the shadows. But the fight didn't begin with IJP, or InterACT, or even ISNA. Like a supernova, it started a long time ago, when the first intersex people were born and survived and made their marks on this world, and only now are we beginning to see the light from those earlier explosions. The cumulative ruptures of all these acts of resistance are reaching through space-time and being felt today.

But Amira and Kamoorah didn't share my enthusiasm for the wonders of space. They stared back at me with blank expressions.

"You're silly, Pidgeon," Amira said.

"Is you a boy or a girl, Pidgeon?" Kamoorah asked.

I'd gotten used to educating people about intersex identity in my daily life, but I hadn't talked all of this through with my new neighbors yet. "I was born both," I said. "And each day, I wake up and decide if I want to be a boy or a girl that day."

"What did you decide today?" Amira asked.

I looked down and realized I was looking rather girly that day.

"Today, I'm a girl."

"So tomorrow you might wake up and decide you're a boy?" Kamoorah excitedly asked.

"Yeah."

"That's so cool!" Amira said.

"Is that why you have a mustache on your face?" Kamoorah then asked.

"No, that's just because my family is hairy." I chuckled.

Then Amira asked, "Can we come visit the chicks tomorrow?"

"Of course you can. You can visit them whenever you want."

ACKNOWLEDGMENTS

To everyone who has ever lent a helping hand, a sympathetic ear, or a shoulder to cry on throughout my journey: thank you.

RESOURCES

Go to pid.ge/resources (or nobodyneedstoknow.com/resources) for an up-to-date list.

A Changing Paradigm: US Medical Provider Discomfort with Intersex Care Practices: a follow-up report by Human Rights Watch in collaboration with Inter/Act

Do's and Don'ts #4intersex Allies: the most important tips for all allies, plus advice specifically for medical allies

IJP's #EndIntersexSurgery Posters: Google Drive folder that includes tutorials for printing and wheat pasting

IJP's "How to Organize an #EndIntersexSurgery" Tool Kit: how to organize an #EndIntersexSurgery protest in your city

interACT's Free Resources: the amazing *What We Wish* brochure series by intersex youth, plus resources for intersex people and their families and medical providers

interACT's Instagram: Be sure to check out the link in their bio! It's chock-full of the latest and greatest resources.

Intersex 101: A Guide to Understanding the Basics of Intersex, **a zine by Banti Jaswal**: Banti is a youth member of interACT (Advocates for Intersex Youth), queer, nonbinary, an intersex person, and an artist. This is a free download.

Intersex-Affirming Hospital Policies: interACT and Lambda Legal's guide to providing ethical and compassionate health care to intersex patients

"I Want to Be Like Nature Made Me": Medically Unnecessary Surgeries on Intersex Children in the US: a report by Human Rights Watch in collaboration with Inter/Act

Supporting Intersex Employees by Inter/Act: You have intersex employees in your workforce. Congratulations! Here's how to support them.

Supporting Intersex Students: A Resource for Students, Families, and Educators: guidance on supporting intersex students from the US Department of Education Office for Civil Rights

Speak Up #4intersex: How to Speak the Language on Social Media: a guide to talking about intersex on social media, hashtags, and language

Media

A Normal Girl: This short documentary brings the widely unknown struggles of intersex people to light through my story as an intersex activist.

I Am Intersex: ILGA and Buzzfeed LGBT hired Antimatter Studio to produce this short and poignant animated video for parents of intersex babies. Voice-over by me!

Intersexions: In this groundbreaking feature documentary, intersex individuals reveal the secrets of their unconventional lives—and how they navigate their way through this strictly male/female world when they fit somewhere in between. (A free version also exists on YouTube and Tubi.)

Organizations

interACT: Advocates for Intersex Youth: interACT uses innovative legal and other strategies to advocate for the human rights of children born with intersex traits.

Intersex Justice Project: Intersex Justice Project works to end invasive and unnecessary surgeries on intersex youth by empowering intersex people of color to make change.

Organization Intersex International: OII is a decentralized global network of intersex organizations.

Support

InterConnect Support Group: a compassionate community of intersex individuals, family members, and trusted allies working together to promote a better quality of life through connection, support, and education

iSpace: a peer-support group and resource *by* and *for* intersex people under thirty, in which all intersex variations, genders, sexualities, backgrounds, and locations are welcome

Books

***Fixing Sex: Intersex, Medical Authority, and Lived Experience* by Katrina Karkazis**: Karkazis offers a nuanced, compassionate picture of these charged issues in the first book to examine contemporary controversies over the medical management of intersexuality in the United States from the perspectives of those most intimately involved.

***Hermaphrodites and the Medical Invention of Sex* by Alice Dreger**: Dreger takes us inside doctors' chambers to see how and why medical and scientific men constructed sex, gender, and sexuality as they did, and especially how the material conformation of hermaphroditic bodies—when combined with social exigencies—forced peculiar constructions.

***Lessons from the Intersexed* by Suzanne J. Kessler**: Kessler's interviews with pediatric surgeons and endocrinologists reveal how the intersex condition is normalized for parents, and she argues that the way in which medical and psychological professionals manage intersexuality displays our culture's beliefs about gender and genitals.

ABOUT THE AUTHOR

Photo © 2023 Sarah Joyce

Pidgeon Pagonis is an activist on behalf of intersex and marginalized people. They have advanced youth advocacy with inter-ACT, launched an intersex YouTube channel, written for *Everyday Feminism*, cofounded the Intersex Justice Project (IJP) and the #EndIntersexSurgery campaign, and introduced the intersex and nonbinary clothing line Too Cute to Be Binary. They've created two short documentaries, *The Son I Never Had*, which premiered at Outfest, and *A Normal Girl*, which screened at the American Pavilion at the Cannes Film Festival; appeared on the cover of *National Geographic's* "Gender Revolution" special issue; and been honored as an LGBT Champion of Change by the Obama White House. They are currently documenting intersex people of color for *Physical Record*, a new photo series subsidized by Astraea's Intersex Human Rights Fund. For more information visit www.pid.ge.